Designing Matrix Organizations That Actually Work

How IBM, Procter & Gamble, and Others Design for Success

Jay R. Galbraith

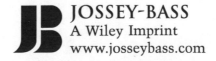

JOSSEY-BASS
A Wiley Imprint
www.josseybass.com

Published by Jossey-Bass
A Wiley Imprint
989 Market Street, San Francisco, CA 94103-1741—www.josseybass.com

Jossey-Bass books and products are available through most bookstores. To contact Jossey-Bass directly call our Customer Care Department within the U.S. at 800-956-7739, outside the U.S. at 317-572-3986, or fax 317-572-4002.

Jossey-Bass also publishes its books in a variety of electronic formats. Some content that appears in print may not be available in electronic books.

Library of Congress Cataloging-in-Publication Data

Galbraith, Jay R.
    Designing matrix organizations that actually work : how IBM, Procter & Gamble, and others design for success/Jay R. Galbraith.
        p.   cm.—(The Jossey-Bass business & management series)
    Includes bibliographical references and index.
    ISBN 978-0-470-31631-3 (cloth)
1. Matrix organization.   2. Corporate culture.   I. Title.
HD58.5.G35   2009
658.4'02—dc22
                                                                2008021043

Printed in the United States of America
FIRST EDITION
HB Printing   10 9 8 7 6 5 4 3 2 1

The Jossey-Bass
Business & Management Series

This book is dedicated to my wife, Sasha.
It is her willingness and ability to read and improve
my writing that helps me immeasurably. Dedicating the book
to her is my way of showing my heartfelt appreciation.

Contents

Preface

On several occasions throughout my career, I have considered writing a book on matrix organizations. Each time I decided not to use "matrix" in the title and wrote about organization design or global organization instead. In the 1970s, matrix was too trendy. I thought that once the backlash set in, the book would stop selling. Unfortunately, I was correct. By the 1980s, it was a common belief that matrix structures do not work. Under these conditions, no one would buy the book to begin with. But throughout the 1980s and 1990s, companies continued to introduce matrix or matrix-like structures. To avoid questions from their bosses, the adopters used other names, such as "multidimensional structures" or even the old "line and staff" nomenclature. I remember a project that I had at Kodak. McKinsey recommended a new strategy and a "shared resource" structure. It was a matrix structure with a new label. My learning from these clients was that matrix is an appropriate organization for many business situations. And when experienced managers face these business situations, they adopt a matrix organization, whatever it is called, to perform the business activities.

Matching a matrix organization to the appropriate situation was part of the challenge; getting it to work was a bigger one. Most managers drew the organization charts, debated where the dotted and solid lines would go, and then announced the new matrix structure to their organization. And in most cases, the structure did not work. (In this book, we will see why.) At one point I was counting the successes and failures. As I remember now, it was one in four that were successes. That is, 75 percent of the attempts failed to meet their objectives, and many actually caused more problems than they solved. It was no wonder that the idea that "matrix does not work" took hold. But I still had data points showing that 25 percent of the attempts were successful. Then one day I was calling on a client who was about to abandon the matrix. At lunch I was talking with a disappointed manager. He said the company had not changed the performance appraisal system or the planning process as I and others had advised. He then said, "You know, it's not that matrix is a failure here. It's that we've failed at matrix." The statement captured many of my experiences. I had seen many instances where matrix was implemented poorly and incompletely. Those same managers who saw that matrix was the right structure were not able or willing to do the hard implementation work to make it a success. So one of my purposes in writing this book is to articulate the practices of those 25 percent who were successful.

This idea that matrix does not work still exists today, even among people who should know better (Bryan and Joyce, 2005). Organization structures do not fail; managements fail at implementing them correctly. For example, in the mid-1990s, Sun Microsystems reorganized from a functional structure to an autonomous divisional structure. Management wanted to create miniature Suns to restore the entrepreneurial spirit of the company's start-up days. So they created divisions for high-end servers, desktop computers, printers, software, services, and so on. There were nine divisions in all. This configuration led them to call the structure Sun and the nine planets. Within a few years, Sun discovered the negatives of this structure. Management found that they had nine different compensation plans, nine accounting systems, nine IT systems, nine sales forces calling on the same customers, and so on. They had nine of everything and escalating overhead. It was almost impossible to move talent from one division to the next. Sun then abandoned the autonomous divisional structure and moved to one similar to its old one. Does this mean that autonomous divisional structures do not work? Of course not. The divisional structure serves United Technologies' and General Electric's diversified strategies very well. Sun simply failed to implement the structure in its specific situation. What was the structure the company moved to? You guessed it, the matrix. Sun increased the strength of HR, finance, and marketing across a reduced number of divisions, forming the typical divisional-functional matrix. It formed a single sales force and matrixed product sales specialists between the global sales organization and the product divisions. So one purpose of this book is to dispel the idea that matrix doesn't work. Certainly there are failures, but they are failures of management.

In the 1990s, I was asked by Ed Schein and Dick Beckhardt to revise my 1973 book. I took the opportunity to write about designing all types of lateral or horizontal organizational forms, including matrix forms. We changed the title to *Competing with Flexible Lateral Organizations*. Whether it was the unappealing title or the decline of the OD Series I am not sure, but the book never caught on.

My current interest began while I was on the faculty at the International Institute for Management Development (IMD) in Lausanne, Switzerland. Each year, IMD ran the CEO Roundtable for the CEOs from those companies that were partners of IMD. In 1998, my colleague Ulrich Steger surveyed these CEOs for the top challenges that they were facing. From their responses he compiled what he called the CEOs' Agenda. Some of the challenges were as expected: globalization, intense price competition, and managing constant change. But one was unexpected: it was termed "managing organizational complexity." My colleagues asked me to handle this topic on the agenda. IMD then set up about ten interviews with CEOs and their leadership teams for my preparation. What they told me was that the customer was the new source of complexity. The ABB team said that DaimlerChrysler pointed out to them that there were thirty-seven sales forces from ABB calling on the company. DaimlerChrysler was getting thirty-seven different levels of service from these sales forces, whose members did not know each other. The company asked ABB for a single strong interface. Nokia Networks was facing a consolidating customer base as telecom operators were acquiring each other. IBM's customers were requesting IT solutions rather than buying stand-alone products and integrating them themselves. In all cases, these companies were creating global account teams and gathering them into customer segment units. The complexity came from the fact that they were already struggling to manage through three-dimensional matrix structures of global business units, regions and countries, and global functions. And now customers were requiring a fourth dimension— customers—to be added to these global structures.

I have written about designing these complex organizations in *Designing the Global Corporation* (2000) and *Designing the Customer-Centric Organization* (2005). My intention was to address the complexity that derived from the new customer dimension. But as a result of this focus, I did not address the matrix organization specifically, nor did I title either of the books *Matrix Organization Design*.

But today I am sensing a renewed interest in matrix organizations. I conduct a lot of workshops for the in-house organization design groups that are appearing in an increasing number of companies. I usually tailor the sessions to the interests of the company. When I ask for the topics the managers want addressed, matrix is always on the list. Usually it takes the form of "How do we make a matrix work?" My interpretation of these requests is that we may have turned the corner on matrix. It is no longer a structure to be avoided. Instead it is a necessary form of organization in today's business environment. So the issue today is "How do we learn how to operate the matrix effectively?" Thus it seems to me that a book focusing on how to make a matrix work may finally be a timely contribution.

Indeed, there are still a lot of managers who do not know how to make a matrix work. The following quote is from the (now former) CEO of ABB, Fred Kindle, who responded to a case writer's question about what he thought of ABB's matrix under prior CEOs:

> "For me, [the old ABB] was like the famous movie—*The Matrix*. Total confusion. Nobody knows what is going on, and I don't like that. Most important is clarity and to some extent simplicity. I am absolutely willing to trade in a 100% perfect—academically perfect—but complex organization for only [a] 70% perfect organization that is simple and easy to understand."

> He [the CEO] recalled an instance when he asked his team whether they knew to whom the country manager of Denmark reported. The answer was correct—Zürich—but nobody could name the executive. (Pucik and Zalan, 2007, p. 11)

Here we have a top executive espousing a typical view that matrix doesn't work because it creates confusion and lack of clarity. Now, if there is confusion and lack of clarity about roles and responsibilities in an organization, my question is, "Whose fault is that?" In my view, it is the leader's fault because he or she does not define the roles and processes through which decisions get made. In Chapter Five, I review responsibility charts, which are used in successful matrix implementations. Every consulting firm now promotes its own similar tool. Confusion is not inherent in a matrix. It is, however, often found in poorly implemented matrix organizations. I am sure that if you went to Procter & Gamble, IBM, Nokia, or Toyota, the head of Western Europe in these companies would know the executive to whom the country manager of Denmark reports. It is clear that this former ABB CEO has no idea how an effective matrix works. I am sure that he has never seen or experienced one. It is for managers like this that I wrote this book.

The other astonishing concept expressed in the quote is that the CEO is willing to accept 70 percent of the ideal to get simplicity. Matrix organizations are all about achieving two or more diametrically opposed goals and doing them both well at the same time. The goal is to execute a strategy that is both global *and* local. Or it is striving to deliver new products on compressed time frames *and* to achieve functional excellence. I cannot conceive of General Electric or Procter & Gamble or Toyota settling for 70 percent. Leadership in a matrix is all about mastering the requisite complexity to attain the 100 percent. The quote serves to highlight what it takes to lead a successful matrix organization. Again, one needs to understand what a matrix really is and what the challenges are in order to execute it successfully.

This book is based on my experiences of studying and consulting with matrix organizations for forty years. I started in summer 1967 studying the commercial airplane division of Boeing. Since then, I have worked with computer companies, consumer goods companies, commercial banks, investment banks, telecoms, retailers, semiconductor companies, aerospace firms, Internet companies, and hospitals, among others. I have worked with companies from most countries in Europe, Japan, Latin America, Israel, Indonesia, and the Middle East, as well as North America. Each industry, each country, and each company has its own unique features, but there are some core concepts that make up the content of this book. These concepts are taken from past books, my current workshop notes, and from my most recent experiences.

The book follows the Star Model that I have used in all my books. In the Introduction, I present the definition of matrix organizations, why they are chosen, and why there were failures initially. One of the reasons is that the changes were structure-only. Few companies introduced a complete organization design. The successful ones did implement a complete design. For me a complete design follows the Star Model, with aligned changes in structure, processes, rewards, and people practices. So an explanation of the Star Model completes the introductory chapter.

The book is written in three parts. Part One presents the simple two-dimensional matrix and its variations. The first chapter focuses on the two-dimensional model and looks at two examples of the functional-divisional model: Time-Warner and

Procter & Gamble. Chapters Two and Three describe variations on the matrix theme. Chapter Two focuses on the two-hat model, and Chapter Three focuses on the baton pass model. Chapters Four and Five complete Part One. Chapter Four describes the design issues that companies face when a matrix exists at several levels. This challenge is called the matrix within a matrix. Chapter Five describes some tools for balancing power between the two sides of the matrix. It includes responsibility charts for defining roles as well.

Part Two focuses on the more complex designs. We begin in Chapter Six with the business unit, geography, and functional three-dimensional design. Chapter Seven describes more complex forms, including the front-back model, which is replacing the three-dimensional global matrix in many situations. Chapter Eight describes IBM's version of the front-back in some detail.

Part Three completes our discussion of the Star Model by presenting the planning processes, reward systems, and HR practices of successful implementers of the matrix. Chapter Nine focuses on the key communication practices. The planning and coordination processes are featured in Chapters Ten and Eleven. Chapter Twelve is devoted to the HR practices and rewards systems needed to reinforce the matrix behaviors. Leadership is key when implementing a matrix; Chapter Thirteen gives advice on the leader's behaviors. Chapter Fourteen presents some approaches to managing the change process when implementing the matrix. In Chapter Fifteen I list the capabilities that companies need to implement a matrix successfully. They are mentioned individually throughout the book, but here I have gathered them together in one place as a summary. Matrix was one of those management practices that was initially hyped and then fell from grace. The Epilogue presents stories of what I have experienced in the use and abuse of the matrix.

Breckenridge, Colorado   Jay R. Galbraith
August 2008

Introduction

MATRIX ORGANIZATIONS

What Are They?
Where Did They Come From?

Why would a company choose a matrix type of organization structure and risk confusing people, such as those who have two bosses? It does so because its business strategies require it to be excellent simultaneously at two or three different things. For example, a business may need to create state-of-the-art technologies and then combine them rapidly into winning products. Strong functional or skill-specialty organizations foster new technologies and technical excellence. They attract talented people to the specialty and give them specialty careers. Yet competition requires the fast combination of specialties into new products and rapid time to market. The ability to meet these product development requirements is fostered by strong product or project managers. When company strategies require both technical excellence and fast time to market, a matrix of products and specialties results.

A multinational company may require excellence in global integration, local responsiveness, and functional skills. These companies require both global integration within a business and local responsiveness within a country. The global business unit coordinates across countries, and the country manager coordinates across businesses. The company does not want to choose between being global *or* being local. It wants to be global when launching new products and local when serving customers. Again, a matrix organization results when the company's strategy requires both outcomes. The price of achieving both outcomes simultaneously is having to deal with the complexity of managing in a two-boss structure.

One of the main drivers for choosing a matrix structure is the pursuit of a dual- or multiple-priority strategy. The multinational company places equal priority on being global and on being local. It may pursue multiple priorities if it also requires functional excellence. A high-technology company like Nokia will want excellence in R&D and supply chain. Nokia values its brand and will want marketing excellence. These strategic intentions are implemented by having a talented person in charge of these functions. These functional people as well as global businesses and local geographies will report to the CEO or someone else high in the organization's structure. A matrix structure results.

The other reason for choosing a matrix structure is the sharing of specialized and expensive resources. If the aforementioned business put all the specialists in the product organizations, it could achieve fast time to market. But specialists like to work in functional structures. And dedicating specialists to specific products is expensive. Companies usually want to avoid duplication and to be able to move people and ideas across products. The need to have strong product units that share functional specialists is another driver for adopting a matrix structure. Or the resource could be very expensive. It costs around $3 billion for a silicon fabrication facility today. Each business unit cannot afford its own. Instead the silicon fabs are in a separate unit and matrixed across the businesses.

I've written this book for two reasons. First, it is still a challenge to get a matrix organization to work smoothly. More and more managers are saying, "We have to learn how to make a matrix work." These managers have learned that managing in a matrix is an essential capability that their company needs to learn. This book is intended to provide the guidance for building that capability. Second, there will be an increasing number of situations where matrix will be the organization of choice. All repetitive, well-understood types of work will be automated, go into software, or be outsourced to low-cost countries. The work left in our organizations will be professional work. It is this professional work that is appropriate for matrix types of organization. The bottom line is that we need to learn how to design matrix organizations that can function effectively.

In this Introduction, I first define what I mean by a matrix organization and give some examples. Then I briefly trace the origins of matrix up to the present time. Finally I present the Star Model, which will guide the complete design of the matrix type of organization. The rest of the book will examine the structures, processes, and HR practices that support a well-functioning matrix design.

What Is a Matrix?

A matrix is a type of organization structure that is built around two or more dimensions, such as functions, products, or regions, and in which people have two bosses. The structure shown in Figure I.1 is an example.

The figure shows two dimensions reporting to the R&D lab director. One dimension is the skill-specialty groups, such as electronics and software. The second dimension is projects that use the talent in the specialty groups in a changing array of R&D projects. The figure shows two projects for the automotive and the aerospace product lines. In each specialty group, there is a subproject manager who manages the project and the talent within the specialty group. The figure shows that there are two subproject managers in each specialty, one for auto and one for aero. This subproject manager reports to both the skill-specialty manager and to the project manager. This dual reporting is one of the defining characteristics of matrix organizations. It means that the subproject manager gets direction from both bosses. The dual reporting is also intended to imply a roughly equal power balance between the two sides of the matrix. This balance of power is the other defining characteristic of the matrix organization. Usually there is

Figure I.1: A Matrix Structure of Specialists and Projects in an R&D Lab

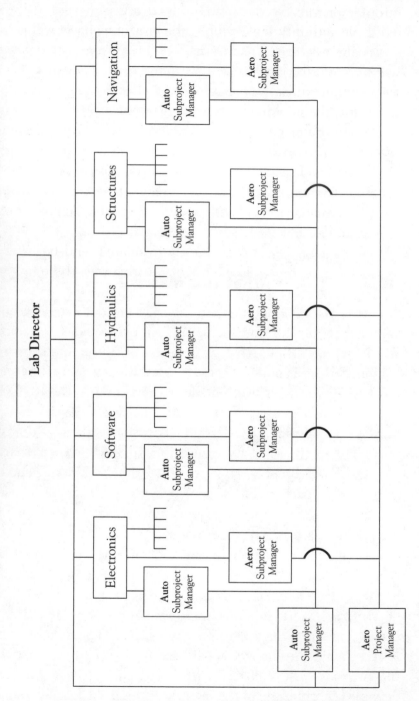

an attempt to carve out separate areas in which the two bosses will have authority. For example, the project manager will usually determine *what* to do and *when* to do it. The specialist manager will have jurisdiction over *how* to do the work. There is still overlap between the areas, but attempts to define areas of authority will clarify the situation and minimize disputes.

When the matrix is working well, the two bosses communicate with each other to detect issues early and prevent unnecessary conflicts. Usually they jointly select the person to be the subproject manager. They then agree on a set of goals against which the manager will be evaluated. This agreement minimizes giving conflicting goals to the manager with two bosses. The subproject manager is then jointly evaluated, and both bosses sign off on the performance review. In this way, the subproject manager reports to two bosses.

A couple of other common examples are shown in Figures I.2 and I.3.

Figure I.2: Typical Corporate Structure with Business Unit CFO Reporting to the Business Unit and CFO

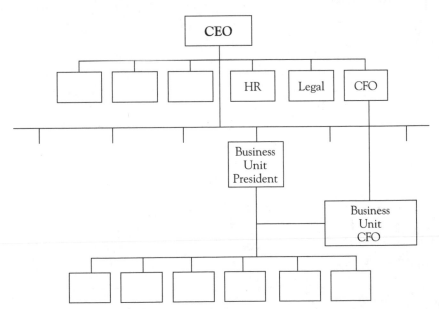

Figure I.3: Multibusiness, Multinational Matrix

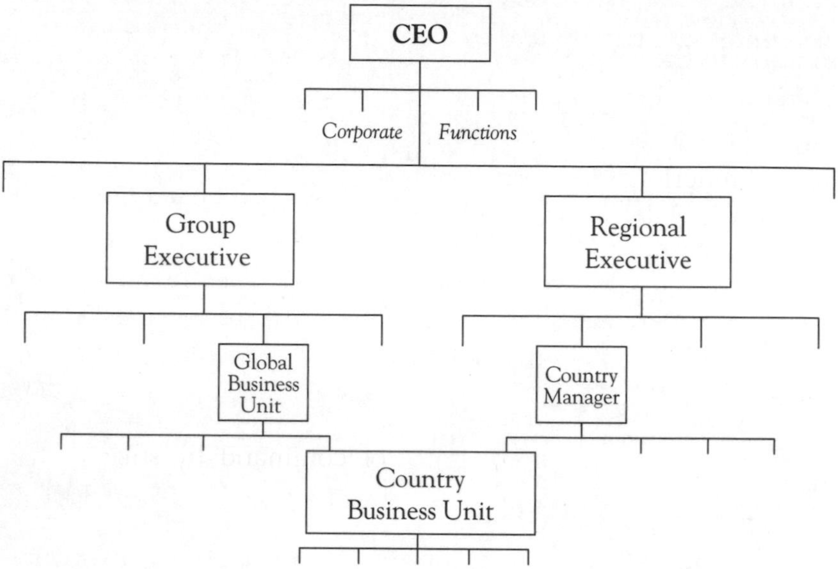

In Figure I.2 is a matrix structure in a multibusiness corporation. Typically the functions (finance, HR, legal, and so on) report to the business unit president and to the corporate functional vice president. The finance function is shown in Figure I.2. Another common example is in international structures. Figure I.3 shows a multibusiness, multinational corporation's structure. In this company, there are many businesses that are clustered into groups, sometimes called sectors. When the company is present in a large number of countries, the countries are grouped into regions. This structure then has two levels between the CEO and the manager with two bosses. In Figure I.2, there is only one level. The examples show the variations that are possible. In general, the fewer the layers between the two-boss manager and the leader who can resolve disputes, the better the matrix will function.

What Are the Origins of the Matrix?

In my view, the modern matrix emerged from the aerospace industry in the 1960s. However, it has its origins in the Scientific Management era of the early 1900s. It was Frederick Taylor who suggested the benefits of having multiple bosses. His idea was labeled functional foremanship. He suggested that the workforce have a schedule boss, a quality boss, a tool boss, an administrative boss, and so on. He wanted to bring specialist skills directly to the workforce. No one else liked this idea because of the confusion of multiple bosses.

The acceptable position was articulated in 1917 by Henri Fayol ([1949] 1987). He described the line-and-staff model. He underlined the concept of unity of command by stating that every employee should have one and only one boss. In addition, authority should run in an unbroken line from the leader at the top to the workers at the bottom. Together these ideas specify a hierarchy of authority as the preferred organizational form. This hierarchy was the line organization. However, he liked the idea of bringing expertise to bear through specialist roles. But these specialist roles, called staff roles, had no authority. They would provide advice and service when requested by the line managers in the hierarchy. When the line managers were persuaded by the staff, the line and not the staff would issue the expert advice as their command. Only the line could issue official orders. This model preserved the unity-of-command principle yet allowed expert advice to be used.

In practice, the line-and-staff model was never as clear as Fayol's presentation of it. For example, the finance function shown in Figure I.2 would often act as if it were in command. When a company was financially stressed or when there was some accounting chicanery in the field, the communication from the CFO seemed less like advice and more like an order. However, the fiction of unity of command was always maintained. In the 1960s, that fiction was confronted in aerospace.

The aerospace industry grew rapidly after Russia launched *Sputnik* in 1957. A large number of projects were initiated. The Rand Corporation did a study of all these projects in the early 1960s (Peck and Scherer, 1962). It found that these projects met or exceeded their technical targets. Schedule performance was on average 150 percent in excess of the target completion date. Cost and budget performance was an average 320 percent above the initial estimates. These statistics clearly reflected the national priorities. Get the best technology into the field as quickly as possible and spend whatever it takes to meet the number one and two goals. It was a great time to be an aerospace engineer.

In the late 1960s, the national priorities changed. There were simply not enough resources to fund the three big national programs. First there was the space program. Schedules became a priority when Kennedy said "Man on the moon by 1970" (not 1975). Then there was the defense buildup to support the Vietnam War. At the same time, Boeing was growing to dominate the global commercial aircraft market. Following the introduction of the 707 and the 727, Boeing was launching the 737, the 747, and the government-supported Supersonic Transport (SST). When resources are scarce, costs and budgets become priorities. The result was that we still wanted state-of-the-art technology to get to the moon (and back). But aerospace companies had to deliver their projects more cost-effectively and on schedule. These were dual strategic priorities. NASA and the Department of Defense (DOD) changed from cost-plus to incentive contracts. The incentives were for cost and schedule performance outcomes as well as technical performance. There was a time when DOD and NASA even issued fixed-price contracts. It was a new game in aerospace. The change in strategic priorities resulted in changes in the aerospace company organizations. They all adopted matrix structures. They maintained the strong functions, such as engineering, but added a new strong project management organization. Before, projects were run by project coordinators who worked for the vice president of engineering. That structure represented the old priorities. The new dual priorities meant that strong project managers reported to the general manager along with the head of engineering. The structure created a power balance. The project managers became the champions of cost and schedule performance as well as technical performance on their projects. Although making the change was difficult, it was regarded as successful, and it contributed to the success of the NASA lunar landing program. There was a man on the moon before 1970.

The commercial world was initially reluctant to adopt the matrix. It was seen as expensive, and only the government could afford the overhead of the dual structure. But Boeing applied the matrix to its commercial airplane program, which is where I learned matrix from 1967 to 1969 (see Galbraith, 1973, chap. 9). The R&D community also began to adopt it in their labs. (Today matrix is seen as the natural way to run an R&D operation.) From the R&D experience it spread into the rest of the organization, especially for companies competing on new product development. The press then picked matrix up as the hot new idea. Books began to appear. The best was Stan Davis and Paul Lawrence's *Matrix* (1977).

By the late 1970s, however, enough companies were experiencing difficulties that the word spread that "matrix doesn't work." The last nail in the coffin came from Peters and Waterman's *In Search of Excellence* (1982). They claimed that none of the excellent companies used a matrix. The assertion was not true. Intel, Texas Instruments, Digital Equipment, Boeing, Fluor, and Bechtel all used it appropriately in their businesses. But that didn't matter; the coffin was sealed. It would not be until the 1990s that managers could again talk openly in public about using a matrix organization. What happened?

What Happened?

Matrix organization is one of those management concepts, like Total Quality Management (TQM) or reengineering, that became very popular and then went through the management fashion cycle. Coming out of aerospace in the 1960s, matrix became popular in the 1970s and early 1980s. And, as usually happens, matrix in many of these organizations was wrongly adopted, hastily installed, and inappropriately implemented. When performance did not meet expectations, the matrix structure was abandoned. The word quickly spread: "We tried matrix, and it doesn't work." From then on, managers avoided matrix, even in situations where it was appropriate. Then they noticed two things. First, matrix seems to have worked at some companies. Second, they recognized that they faced situations where a matrix would be valuable. At that time, around the mid- to late 1990s, the concept of matrix assumed its normal place in management's toolkit. That is where matrix is today, almost.

Matrix is a collaborative organizational form. I believe it needs to be implemented using a collaborative change process. The people should develop the collaborative skills during implementation that they will need during the full-scale operation. Instead, in the past many matrix structures were introduced through the command-and-control process. People were ordered to collaborate and usually faked it. The parts of the organization that had power were ordered to share it. They usually did not and actively (but usually passively) resisted the introduction of power-sharing arrangements. Then when the outcomes that required power sharing were not achieved, the resistors were quick to point out the failures and to suggest that the matrix organization was not working. So, quite often, poorly managed or unmanaged change processes resulted in failure, even when matrix was appropriate for the business situation.

Very often the company, division, or country did not have the capabilities to support a full-blown matrix structure. For example, if a division was characterized by functional silos, a matrix using product managers would not work. But recommendations to knock down the silos first were not appreciated. The division manager had two years to make his mark. He usually went ahead with a matrix structure anyway, to his chagrin. Thus many matrix organizations were hastily installed rather than carefully built over time.

Matrix was often inappropriately implemented. Once a new management concept becomes "acclaimed," it becomes a tool in company power politics. For example, there were a large number of conglomerates in the 1970s. Except for the finance function, the corporate functions in a conglomerate were "lite" versions of corporate staffs. They were like Fayol's staff roles. They were to deliver advice and service. If a business unit did not request service, the corporate functions were to leave it alone. In my opinion, as well as that of others, the lite form of corporate function is the appropriate form in a conglomerate structure. Many conglomerate corporate functions did not see it that way. Instead they invoked the matrix organization as the ideal modern structure. They would say, "We will never be among *Fortune*'s most admired companies unless we adopt the matrix form of organization." Of course the real agenda was a power grab. The functions wanted a dotted or preferably a solid line into their functions within the business units. They could then make mischief in the businesses. Matrix was an ideal tool for these political maneuvers because it dealt directly with the power dimension. But such abuses led to more resistance to the concept of matrix organizations. Indeed matrix was often a politically correct reason for failure and discontinuance of the strong function program.

The other way that matrix organizations were inappropriately installed was that they were incompletely implemented. Most matrix organizations implemented only structural changes. By the time the leaders negotiated the dotted and solid lines, they had little appetite for making changes to the budgeting process or the compensation system. As it turns out, these supporting changes to the process infrastructure are more important to making a matrix work than the dotted-line structure. So when a collaborative matrix structure conflicted with a reward system that promoted individual rather than group efforts, the reward system won every time.

A number of multinational companies initially built their businesses country by country. Then when they introduced global business units, there were no accounting systems to track the performance of a business across countries. Each country had different IT systems, different inventory valuation systems, different depreciation schedules, and so on. There was no way to coordinate these global business units. The power rested with the countries a little longer. So a matrix requires not just dual reporting relations but dual accounting systems to support both sides of the matrix.

The lesson is that changing to a matrix structure requires complementary and reinforcing changes to the IT system, planning and budgeting processes, the performance management system, the bonus awards, the selection and development criteria, and so on. It requires a complete organization redesign. From these lessons, I devised the Star Model (Galbraith, 1977), which I present in the next section. The model is my guide to building organizational capabilities carefully and completely so as to implement a matrix successfully when it is appropriate. The Star Model can be used for any redesign. We will apply it in subsequent chapters to the design of matrix organizations.

The Star Model

The Star Model framework for organization design is the foundation on which a company bases its design choices. The framework consists of a series of design policies that are controllable by management and can influence employee behavior. The policies are the tools with which management must become skilled in order to shape the decisions and behaviors of their organizations effectively.

Figure I.4: The Star Model

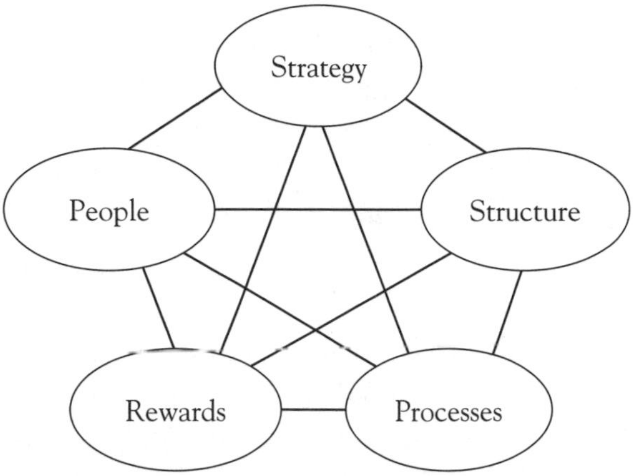

In the Star Model, as shown in Figure I.4, design policies fall into five categories. The first is *strategy*, which determines direction. The second is *structure*, which determines the location of decision-making power. The third is *processes*, which have to do with the flow of information; they are the means of responding to information technologies. The fourth is *rewards* and reward systems, which influence the motivation of people to perform and to address organizational goals. The fifth category of the model is made up of policies relating to *people* (human resource policies), which influence and frequently define the employees' mind-sets and skills.

Strategy

Strategy is the company's formula for winning. The company's strategy specifies the goals and objectives to be achieved as well as the values and missions to be pursued; it sets out the basic direction of the company. The strategy specifically delineates the products or services to be provided, the markets to be served, and the value to be offered to the customer. It also specifies sources of competitive advantage.

Traditionally, strategy is the first component of the Star Model to be addressed. It is important in the organization design process because it establishes the criteria for choosing among alternative organizational forms (see Galbraith, Downey, and Kates, 2002, for tools for translating strategy into criteria). Each organizational form enables some activities to be performed well and hinders others. Choosing organizational alternatives inevitably involves making trade-offs. Strategy is the means by which a company's leaders choose which trade-offs they will accept. Strategy dictates which activities are most necessary and which others are secondary. Matrix organizations result when two or more activities must be accomplished simultaneously without hindering the other. Rather than requiring a company to choose the "or," matrix requires an embracing of the "and." Companies want to be global *and* local.

Structure

The structure of the organization determines the placement of power and authority in the organization. Structure policies fall into four areas:

1. Specialization
2. Shape
3. Distribution of power
4. Departmentalization

Specialization refers to the type and numbers of job specialties used in performing the work. *Shape* refers to the number of people constituting the departments (that is, the span of control) at each level of the structure. Large numbers of people in each department create flat organization structures with few levels. *Distribution of power,* in its vertical dimension, refers to the classic issues of centralization or decentralization. In its lateral dimension, it refers to the movement of power to the department dealing directly with the issues critical to its mission. *Departmentalization* is the basis for forming departments at each level of the structure. The standard dimensions on which departments are formed are functions, products, workflow processes, markets, customers, and geography. Matrix structures are ones in which two or more dimensions report to the same leader at the same level.

Processes

Information and decision processes cut across the organization's structure; if structure is thought of as the anatomy of the organization, processes are its physiology or functioning. Management processes are both vertical and horizontal.

Vertical processes, as shown in Figure I.5, allocate the scarce resources of funds and talent. They are usually business planning and budgeting processes. The needs of different departments are centrally collected, and priorities are decided for the budgeting

Figure I.5: Vertical Processes

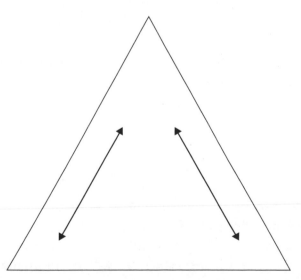

Figure I.6: Horizontal Processes

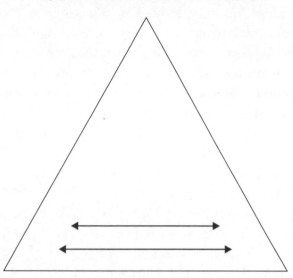

and allocation of the resources to capital, R&D, training, and so on. These management processes are central to the effective functioning of matrix organizations. They need to be supported by dual or multidimensional information systems.

Horizontal processes (also known as lateral processes), as shown in Figure I.6, are designed around the workflow—for example, new product development or the entry or fulfillment of a customer order. These management processes are becoming the primary vehicle for managing in today's organizations. Lateral processes can be carried out in a range of ways, from voluntary contacts between members to complex and formally supervised teams.

Rewards

The purpose of the reward system is to align the goals of the employee with the goals of the organization. It provides motivation and incentive for the employee to carry out the strategic direction. The organization's reward system defines policies regulating salaries, promotions, bonuses, profit sharing, stock options, and so forth. A great deal of change is taking place in this area, particularly as it supports the lateral processes. Companies are now implementing pay-for-skill salary practices, along with team bonuses or gain-sharing systems. There is also the burgeoning practice of offering nonmonetary rewards, such as recognition or challenging assignments.

The Star Model suggests that the reward system must be congruent with the structure and processes to influence the strategic direction. Reward systems are effective only when they form a consistent package in combination with the other design choices.

People

This area governs the human resource (HR) policies of recruiting, selection, rotation, training, and development. HR policies—in the appropriate combinations—produce the talent required by the strategy and structure of the organization, generating the skills and mind-sets necessary to implement its chosen direction. Like the policy choices in the other areas, these policies work best when consistent with the other connecting design areas.

HR policies also build the organizational capabilities to execute the strategic direction. Flexible organizations require flexible people. Cross-functional teams require people who are generalists and who can cooperate with each other. Matrix organizations need people who can manage conflict and can influence without authority. HR policies simultaneously develop people and organizational capabilities.

Implications of the Star Model

As the layout of the Star Model illustrates, structure is only one facet of an organization's design. This is important—most design efforts invest far too much time drawing the organization chart and far too little on processes and rewards. Structure is usually overemphasized because it affects status and power, and a change to it is most likely to be reported in the business press and announced throughout the company. However, in a fast-changing business environment, and in matrix organizations, structure is becoming less important, while processes, rewards, and people are becoming more important.

Another insight to be gained from the Star Model is that different strategies lead to different organizations. Although this seems obvious, it has ramifications that are often overlooked. There is no one-size-fits-all organization design that all companies—regardless of their particular strategy needs—should subscribe to. There will always be a current design that has become "all the rage." But no matter the fashionable

Figure I.7: Organization Design Affects Behavior

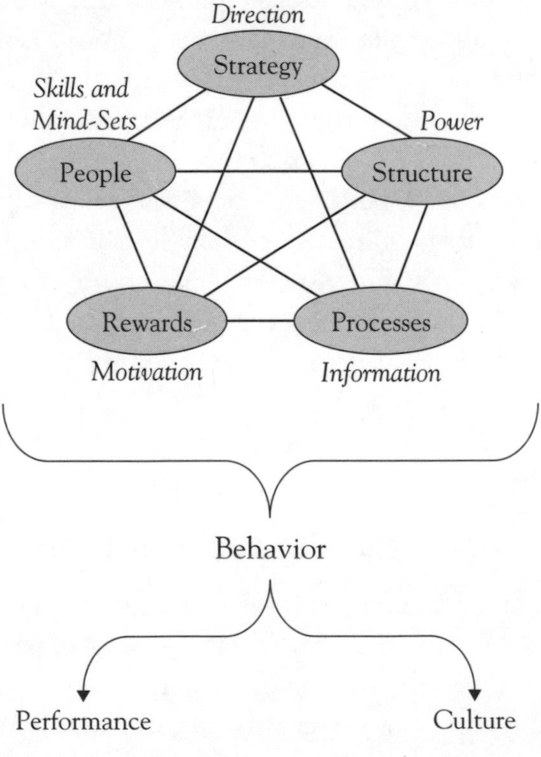

design—whether it is the matrix design or the virtual corporation—trendiness is not sufficient reason to adopt an organization design. All designs have merit, but not for all companies in all circumstances. The design—or combination of designs—that should be chosen is the one that best meets the criteria derived from the strategy.

A third implication of the Star Model is in the interweaving nature of the lines that form the star shape. For an organization to be effective, all the policies must be aligned, interacting harmoniously with one another. An alignment of all the policies will communicate a clear, consistent message to the company's employees.

The Star Model consists of policies that leaders can control and that can affect employee behavior, as suggested in Figure I.7. It shows that managers can influence performance and culture—but only by acting through the design policies that affect behavior.

Part One

SIMPLE MATRIX
ORGANIZATIONS

In the Introduction, we saw several types of matrix structures. In this first part of the book, we will explore more deeply the simple or two-dimensional structure. This type was the first to emerge out of the aerospace industry in the 1960s and the R&D labs in the 1970s. There have been several variations of the simple type that have emerged for different circumstances. We will examine them in the first three chapters of this part. Chapter One covers the standard matrix design that was illustrated in Figure I.1. We will look at several examples of this standard type for the different types of applications where it has been used.

The next two chapters present two variations on the standard matrix theme. The first is the two-hat model. Some organizations cannot afford the overhead of having a set of vice presidents for functions and another set for products. But because the company still wants a dual focus, it uses the two-hat model, which has one set of vice presidents, each of whom wears two hats. That is, each vice president is responsible for a function and for a product. Sometimes the two-hat model is a transition step, and sometimes it is the model that is used to run a matrix organization. Chapter Two describes the model used by Chrysler before its acquisition by Daimler-Benz.

Another variation on the two-dimensional matrix is the baton pass model, described in Chapter Three. The model is used when there are long product development and life cycles. An example is in consumer packaged goods, with such brands as Kraft mayonnaise or Colgate toothpaste. They will go through cycles in which a new generation of product is created and launched. After launch there is the full implementation to all countries and through all channels. After several years, the product is renewed and relaunched. During the renewal, the product team is led by a manager from R&D up until the launch. Then, during and after the launch, the leadership—the baton—is passed to a product manager in marketing. During the next cycle, the baton is passed again to the manager in R&D. In the pharmaceutical industry there are longer cycles. There is a leader and a team in discovery, which hands off to another leader and team in development, which runs the clinical trials. At launch the product responsibility is passed to a third leader and team to realize the demand in all countries. So there are three teams and two baton passes. The pharmaceutical example is described in Chapter Three.

Chapter Four focuses on the situation in which a matrix is replicated at successive levels of the structure. This situation is referred to as the matrix within a matrix. For example, there is a CFO role at the corporate center, at the second level of the international division, and also at the third or country level. There will be a matrix at the international and the country levels for the finance function. Some of the alternatives are explored in the chapter.

The design of the two-dimensional matrix is intended to achieve a power balance between the two dimensions. In reality it is not necessary to achieve a razor's-edge balance. A rough balance will usually suffice. But what is necessary is for the leader to have the skill to change the power situation to continually maintain the balance. Chapter Five describes the various power levers that the leader can control and should master. One of the levers is the responsibility chart, which can be used to change decision rights across the matrix. The chapter describes the use of the charts in detail.

In Part Two, I describe the more complex matrix designs—three-dimensional or four-dimensional structures, as well as structures with even more dimensions.

1

SIMPLE MATRIX STRUCTURES

In this first chapter, we focus on the two-dimensional matrix structure. This two-dimensional model was the first to appear and is still a frequently occurring structure. In its first appearance, the two-dimensional model was not even called a matrix. It was referred to as the line-and-staff model. But as the model was used in aerospace in the 1960s and in R&D labs in the 1970s, the term *matrix* was applied. The term has been used for all two-dimensional models ever since. We begin our discussion with a number of different applications.

Two-Dimensional Structures

The two-dimensional structure arises frequently in all organizations. We have already seen one example of an R&D lab in Figure I.1 in the Introduction. In the next section, we discuss the typical corporate function–profit center matrix that is common to all corporate centers. Despite a long history, this application can still generate arguments about who has the solid line and who has the dotted line. We will use this example to discuss the phenomenon of dotted lines.

The next example is of a sales organization. Sales today is one of the most complex organizations in the company. We will start with the simple geographic and national account matrix structure.

Corporate Functions

No matter what the profit centers are in a company, there is the usual matrix of corporate functions and profit centers.

These profit centers could form a regional structure (Nestlé), a customer segment structure (American Express), or a business unit structure (United Technologies). In all cases, there is at least a finance function led by the chief financial officer (CFO) who reports to the CEO, and finance leaders who report to the profit-and-loss (P&L) leaders as well as the CFO. The labels may vary, but there will be such other functions as HR, legal, strategy, and external affairs, which are structured in the same way.

There might be just a few functions, as in a holding company or conglomerate structure, or many, as in a related divisional structure. Figure 1.1 shows the Time Warner (TW) structure. TW operates as a holding company with very independent businesses. The holding company corporate center contains just a few corporate functions. These functions have a dotted-line relationship with their counterparts in the businesses. That is, the functions in the businesses report first to the business unit manager ("solid line") and second to the corporate function ("dotted line").

The Procter and Gamble (P&G) structure is a contrast to the TW structure. P&G has numerous corporate functions that play a strong role in the conduct of the enterprise. The P&G corporate structure is shown in Figure 1.2. P&G has the same standard corporate functions (HR, CFO, strategy, legal, external affairs) as TW. These functions are standard in both holding companies and divisionalized companies. But P&G also has corporate functions for the operating functions that make up the business units. These units set policy for the function, take ownership for key processes, plan for the future development of the function, and take responsibility for the assignment and development of the functional talent. The P&G corporate functions play a much more influential role than the corporate functions play in a holding company.

The top structure at P&G can be easily determined from the listing of corporate officers in the company's annual report. However, P&G does not publish organization charts showing

Figure 1.1: Time Warner Corporate Matrix Structure (Holding Company)

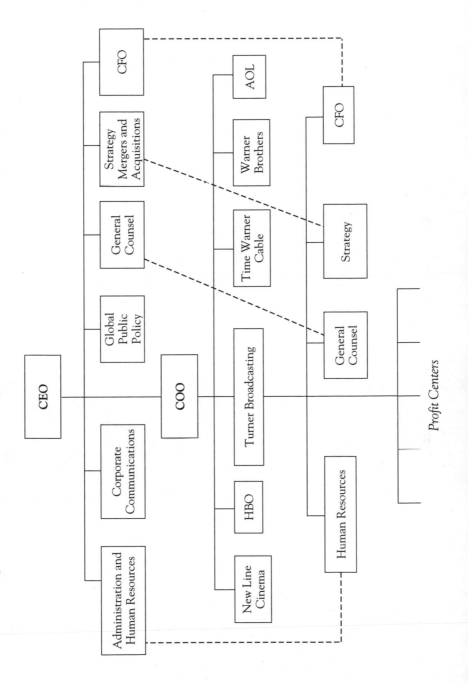

Figure 1.2: Procter & Gamble Corporate Matrix Structure

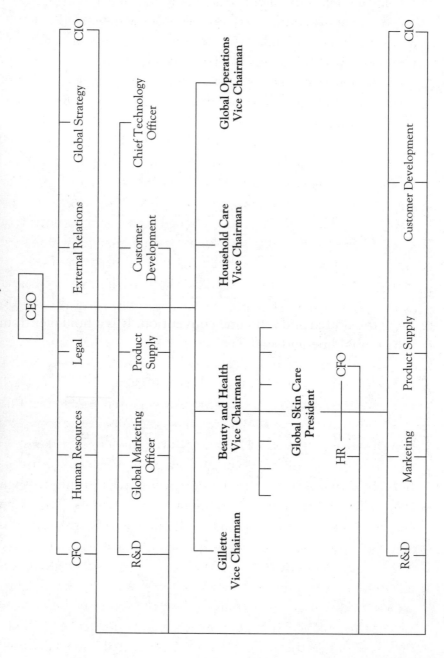

dotted and solid lines. At least I have never seen one. Nor have I heard people talk about solid or dotted-line reporting. So I asked one of my contacts at P&G about how they handle dotted and solid lines. He said, "The last time I even asked one of my two bosses which line was solid and which was dotted, he glared at me and growled 'They're both solid!!' That was about twenty years ago, and I haven't asked since." Today people refer to their line boss and their functional boss. Their line boss gives the performance reviews and operational direction. The functional boss is responsible for career development and functional direction. From my point of view, this is a healthy practice. Enormous amounts of time can be wasted in debates about reporting relationships. I have never seen a change from solid to dotted or vice versa solve the CEO's problem. It only changes which boss is the one who gets upset. It is clearly a win-lose discussion. I much prefer to use responsibility charts (Chapter Five) and shared goals (Chapter Ten). But many companies still insist on using the dotted and solid line convention. It is a holdover from the original line-and-staff days.

These corporate functions were initially called staff roles, which meant that they had no formal authority. Over time, however, it was recognized that these roles were often very influential. The roles had power and influence, but could not have the type of power that we call authority. It was always preferred to maintain the principle of unity of command. At some point, the convention arose that staff roles had a dotted-line relationship to their staff colleagues working for the profit center leaders. The profit centers or line organization had a solid line or authority relationship with those same staff functional roles. The solid line came to mean that the line manager was the real boss. So if there was a conflict between the staff leader's direction and the line leader's direction, the subordinate should follow the solid-line boss's view. Under this practice, the subordinate could be influenced by both bosses as long as there was no conflict. The solid line would then be used when there was a conflict.

A number of different practices have evolved over time for dealing with the two bosses. Today there are standard ways to talk about these practices. One was mentioned in the Introduction. Often the line boss will determine what activities will be performed and when they will be performed. The corporate functional boss will determine how the activities will be performed. This practice is useful, but there can still be conflicts. The solid line is again the conflict resolver. Other practices are used to maintain the power balance. One convention is that the dotted line goes to the boss with whom the subordinate is physically located. The solid line goes to the remote boss to compensate for the lack of day-to-day contact. Another convention is that the dotted line goes to the boss who has the responsibility for the subordinate's next career move. The solid line to the other boss is to maintain the power balance.

In all cases in the past, the solid-line boss made the determination on performance and submitted the salary increase and bonus request. In many cases, the solid-line boss had to collect input from the dotted-line boss but still made the final performance recommendation. Today the performance and talent management decisions are being made by a group that might be referred to as the management development committee. The purpose is to arrive at a full and fair assessment of the employee's performance (Chapter Twelve). Many of the practices that are implied by the solid line are being superseded by more modern and matrix-friendly practices. These will be discussed in later chapters.

Sales Organization Matrix

The matrix structure arises in many places throughout an organization. Figure 1.3 shows an example of a simple structure for a sales organization.

Sales organizations are usually regionally organized to minimize travel costs and have local salespeople call on local buyers.

Figure 1.3: Regional-National Account Matrix

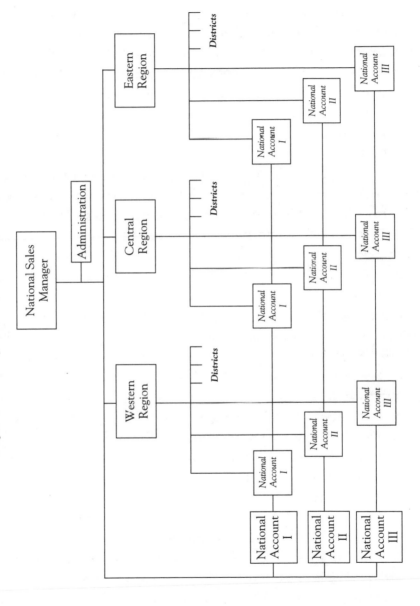

But there are often a few large national, even global, accounts. These customers ask for a single interface and often a single contract from their vendors. But these large accounts still need local salespeople to call on their national account's local offices throughout the country. The result is a regional–national account matrix, as shown in Figure 1.3. It is a simple matrix because it has only two dimensions, regions and customer accounts, and there is only one level of organization between the two-boss manager—the national account representative in the region (shown here as national account I)—and the national sales manager who can resolve disputes.

This model is the simple matrix structure. Disputes can be raised rapidly through one level and quickly be resolved. There are two, not three or four, sides to the issues. The leader is usually in touch with the issues. If need be, the national sales manager can call everyone into a room, hold a face-to-face discussion, and arrive at a decision. If there are more levels, the decision process becomes more complex. It is harder to raise an issue through two levels to the leader, in this case the national sales manager. When more levels are involved, it is more likely that distorted and different versions of the issue will come to the leader. The leader gets farther away from the day-to-day issues. In a two-level organization, if the leader calls everyone in a room, about fifty people will probably show up. The leader can still call the nine people involved in a dispute if he or she can identify the right nine actors. You can still manage a two-level matrix. However, I always discourage companies from using more than two levels, particularly if the people are scattered around the world. It is just not worth the trouble. I have seen only a few three-level matrix structures that work effectively.

An overly layered structure can often be redesigned to reduce levels. Figure 1.4 (A) is a matrix structure with too many layers. The company has a single sales organization for large accounts that buy from several business units. Each business unit has its own specialized sales force. Some customers buy

Figure 1.4: Reducing Multiple Layers to Two Layers in a Sales Structure

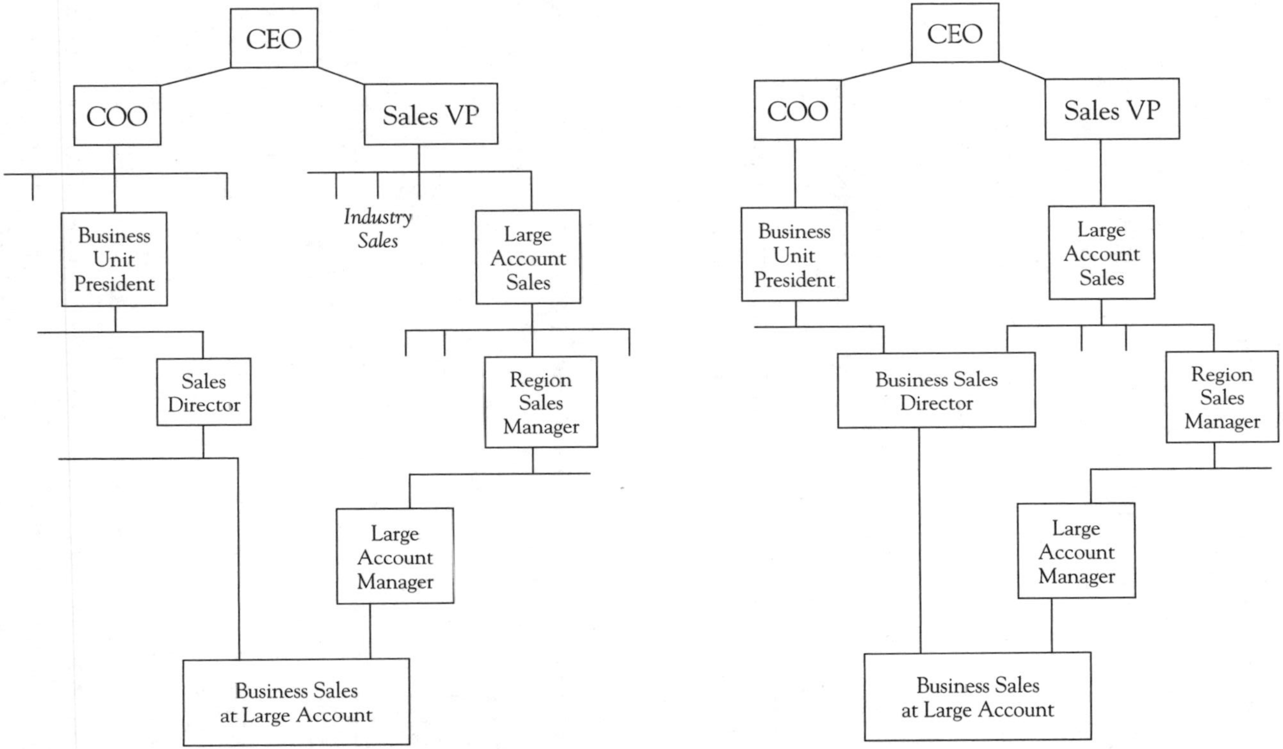

(A) Before

(B) After

from only one business. Through the business unit side, there are three layers between the CEO and the salesperson who represents a business in a large account. These are the COO, the business unit president, and the sales director. On the sales side, there are four levels of management. If there is a dispute between the business sales director and the large account manager concerning the salesperson's time, the issue has to go through two and three levels of management to the CEO. The large number of layers to the CEO means that disputes will be raised reluctantly or not at all. Those issues that are raised will proceed slowly to the CEO's office. The dispute resolution process will be defective with this many levels.

An alternative structure is shown in Figure 1.4 (B). The large account manager can supervise more of the sales force, making the entire sales force operate more as a single sales organization. The business unit sales organizations report to both the large accounts manager and to the business unit president. This structure allows more sales disputes to be resolved at the lower level. These disputes will be resolved more quickly and by people knowledgeable about the sales issues. Big issues between the business unit president and the large account manager can still go to the CEO if needed. So the principle is to position the dispute resolution role as close as possible to the two-boss manager level.

The other reason the matrix structure is simple is that there are only two dimensions, geographic regions and customer accounts. However, computer companies today have product specialists who sell only hardware, another group that sells software, and a third group that sells services. Sales take place through the direct sales force but also through channel partners, such as resellers, the Internet, eBay, systems integrators, and so forth. So computer companies have at least a four-dimensional sales organization because they add products and channels to the two dimensions shown in the simple model in Figure 1.3. I do not discourage companies from adopting the multidimensional matrix. A company's organization must be as complex as its business. If a company is multiproduct, multichannel, multicountry, and multi–customer segment, its organization must also reflect those same four dimensions. In this case, the company needs to master the complexity better than its competitors do. We will deal with multiple dimensions later in Part Two.

Pharmaceutical R&D Lab Example

Pharmaceutical research takes place in two stages, discovery and development. The purpose of the discovery phase is to find a chemical compound that shows desirable effects—some potential in treating a disease state in a human—when it is screened or tested. The development phase takes the most promising compounds from discovery and subjects them to human testing, the last test being the extensive clinical trials. Upon FDA approval of the clinical trial results, the compound is launched into the market. In this section, we examine the change to the matrix organization that the pharmaceutical labs went through in the 1990s. Research studies comparing different company labs show that those laboratories that developed an integrative capability (a matrix-like organization) performed better than those that did not (Henderson, 1994a).

The organization change was driven by changes in the knowledge base underlying the R&D process. Discovery research was initially referred to as a random process during which thousands of compounds were screened. Some came from naturally occurring substances; others were wholly new compounds created by synthetic chemists. The compounds were then injected into diseased rats to see if the compound had the desired effects. When successful, the chemists went to work creating many similar compounds to improve on the compound's desired effects and to eliminate undesirable side effects. This process was called random because the chemists were unaware of the biochemical cause-and-effect relations that would produce the desirable therapeutic response. They would try thousands of compounds until they found some with potential.

The organization consisted of a few specialties that were collected into a functional structure. The synthetic chemists were the central function who handed their compounds to the pharmacologists. The pharmacologists tested the compounds in rats that were managed by the animal biologists or in test tubes run by analytical chemists. The pharmacologists communicated the results to the synthetic chemists, who in turn created more compounds. The communication links were simple sequential ones between the chemists and the pharmacologists. Most of the relevant information was inside the firm. A firm's real asset was its portfolio of potentially effective compounds.

This random process has now been replaced by a rational process based on designing compounds that will have the desired effect on the diseased tissue or malfunctioning organs. Underlying this change were the enormous advances in biochemistry, molecular biology, genetics, physiology, and the life sciences in general. Scientists were now able to understand the chemical reactions leading to high blood pressure, for example. They could understand the molecular structures and the chemical reactions. They could chemically screen the potential compounds without extensive use of animal subjects. But when there is an explosion of knowledge, there is usually an accompanying explosion of specialists who are experts in ever narrower knowledge areas.

The organizations that were implemented to conduct the new rational research were much more complex. In addition to the synthetic chemists, analytical chemists, biologists, and pharmacologists who populated the old lab, molecular biologists, biochemists, metabolic biologists, molecular kineticists, combinatorial chemists, geneticists, computer modelers, and specialists in bio-informatics staffed the new labs. These specialists needed to coordinate and communicate among themselves to design and screen new compounds. In other words, the new discovery lab had more players, and these players were more interdependent. The next challenge was, "How do we coordinate this new complexity?" The answer was to introduce project managers who could lead product teams and coordinate the specialties around promising compounds. These project managers were then organized into product groups, called therapeutic areas—for example, cardiology, central nervous system, infectious diseases, and oncology (cancer). These product groups and teams formed a matrix structure across the functional specialties. One example of such a structure is shown in Figure 1.5. It shows the two-dimensional structure of functional specialties and therapeutic areas forming teams under a project manager from the therapeutic area.

These interdisciplinary teams integrated knowledge across the specialties and focused it into promising products. The less effective labs maintained their functional organizations or switched completely to product or therapeutic area structures. The functional structures produced new knowledge, but it was not integrated and converted into new products. The product organizations produced new products, but the knowledge base decayed, and they were not able to attract specialist talent.

Henderson's research (1994a, 1994b) also shows that the most effective pharmaceutical labs also created complete and aligned organizations, as predicted by the Star Model. The most effective labs used healthy debate among peers to arrive at priorities and resource allocations. The product teams shared and integrated knowledge around products. The open debates integrated knowledge across the laboratory. Many products and treatments can be applied across therapeutic areas. Remember that Viagra was originally intended as a drug to treat heart disease. As we will see in Chapter Ten management processes characterized by open debate are a necessary means to resolve the conflicts generated in a matrix organization.

Figure 1.5: Pharmaceutical Laboratory Matrix

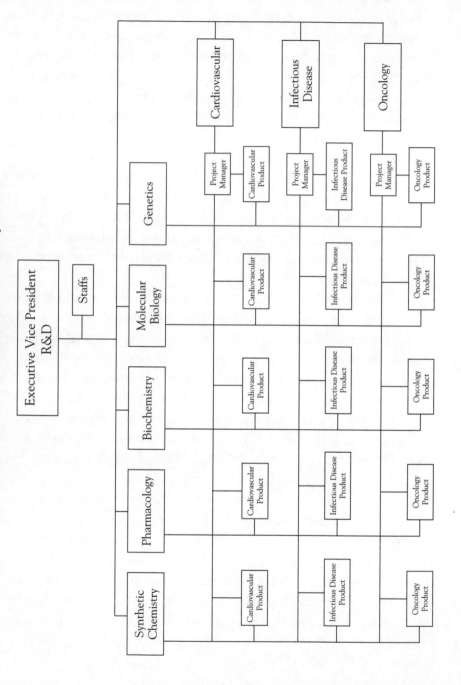

The less effective labs did not use open debate among peers. There was often a lab manager who made all the decisions. This process prevents the lab from learning from the information exchange. Some of the effective labs had leaders who made the tough decisions, but they made the calls after the debate.

The effective labs followed HR policies that attracted, rewarded, and promoted the top scientific talent. These labs encouraged their scientists to publish their research and deliver papers at scientific meetings. They promoted the scientists who had the most publications and had the best reputations in the scientific community. In this way, they attracted the top scientists to the labs. Further, these labs understood that the information to drive the rational process existed outside the lab, and thus ensured that they were integrated into the scientific community and its knowledge resources.

The Star Model shown in Figure 1.6 summarizes our pharmaceutical laboratory example. The change in strategy from the random research process to the rational process was the driving influence of the move away from a functional structure. The new structure was a balance of functions and therapeutic areas in a matrix organization. This new integrated structure was needed to coordinate the larger number of new scientific specialties

Figure 1.6: A Complete and Aligned Matrix Organization

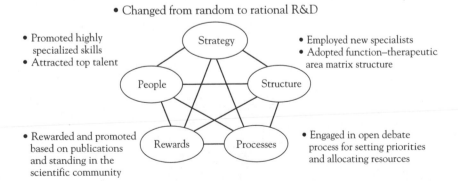

• Changed from random to rational R&D

• Promoted highly specialized skills
• Attracted top talent

Strategy

• Employed new specialists
• Adopted function–therapeutic area matrix structure

People   Structure

• Rewarded and promoted based on publications and standing in the scientific community

Rewards   Processes

• Engaged in open debate process for setting priorities and allocating resources that contributed to the discovery of new compounds. The top performers used management processes characterized by both lively debate and strong decision makers. This process leads to learning and a cross-fertilization of ideas as well as timely resolution of conflicts. The reward system functioned both to attract talented scientists and keep them plugged into their scientific communities. When most of the information exists outside the companies' boundaries, these external linkages are critical.

Summary

This chapter described the simple two-dimensional matrix structure. It arises in many situations throughout a firm. One of the most familiar and oldest examples is the corporate function–profit center matrix. This model varies from the holding company model with a few functions to the divisionalized model with many functions. The P&G model showed strong functions pursuing functional excellence and strong business units integrating across functions for product excellence. The rest of the chapter described some practices involving dotted-line relationships and the number of levels in a matrix. The final example described a high-performing R&D lab in the pharmaceutical industry as following an integrated Star Model.

2

THE TWO-HAT MODEL

Leaders have created several ways of adapting matrix structures to their special needs. In this chapter, we explore the two-hat model. First I describe what it is and give an example. Then we examine why leaders would choose this form of matrix. Surprisingly, there are a number of good reasons why this model makes sense. Finally, we look at some examples, Chrysler's perhaps being the best known.

What Is the Two-Hat Model?

The two-hat model is a common variation of the matrix structure. Let us recall the simple sales matrix shown in Figure 1.3. The two-hat variation is shown in Figure 2.1. It is based on a logic that says, rather than create three new positions for national accounts I, II and III, why not give one account each to the three regional managers? In this way, the three regional managers wear two hats. One hat is on when they manage their region; the other is on when they manage their national account.

There are a number of reasons why companies choose the two-hat model. First, small companies like the model because it saves them the expense of hiring three national account managers. They may be too small to afford the overhead. Small companies probably account for the bulk of the occurrences of the model. Of course, they could hire one national account manager who could manage all three accounts. But this still entails the addition of an expensive role.

There are other reasons for choosing this type of matrix. The model minimizes disputes. Each manager understands the

Figure 2.1: The Two-Hat Matrix Structure

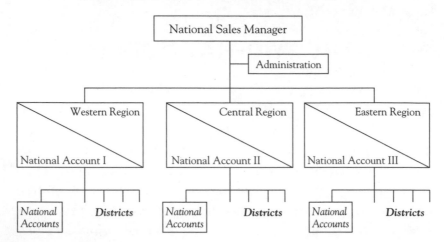

tensions of managing national accounts in his or her region. The model works particularly well when the national accounts actually are headquartered in the managers' regions.

Third, the two-hat model builds stronger teams. The three regional managers are now more interdependent. They share a mutual fate. In fact, it is reciprocity that holds the team together. The implicit message is, "I'll take care of your national account in my region if you take care of my national account in your region." (This idea is also known as mutually assured destruction, or MAD.)

Fourth, the two-hat model is often preferred as a first step toward the full model shown in Figure 1.3. That is, the regional managers often resist the national accounts intrusion in their regions. But if each region gets an account, there is less resistance. The potential resisters become responsible for implementation. They can see the benefits firsthand, and there are fewer turf and territory issues.

I have used the two-hat model for just this reason. The client was a software company with about equal sales in three regions: North America, the United Kingdom, and the rest of the world. As the firm grew, there was a need to organize around three different business models as well. The software business separated into commercial software and large accounts, and consumer software and small businesses. The start-up of a new hosting business created a need for a third business. The regional managers were skeptical about creating three new global business managers, so we implemented a two-hat model. The North American regional manager took the commercial business because most of the large accounts were American companies. The U.K. regional manager took the consumer and small business global unit. And because many small Asian businesses were good candidates for the hosting business, the international region manager took the global hosting business lead. The implementation went smoothly. As the Asian business grew, new regions were created for Asia, Europe, Middle East–Africa, and Latin America. The global hosting business then received a full-time business unit head. With some additional growth, the other regions will be relieved of their second hat. The current regional managers may want to continue running their regions or take a global business role to further their own development.

The fifth reason that the two-hat model is chosen is that it is more acceptable than the alternative (Figure 1.3) in authoritarian cultures. Many people from Latin cultures (for example in Southern Europe and South America) have had great difficulty with matrix structures. However, if the leaders wear two hats, the same leaders will manage with minimal deviation from unity of command and with fewer disputes. Actually, I learned the two-hat model when working with Olivetti in Italy in the 1980s. The company organized very similarly to the aforementioned software company. The two-hat model is probably useful in any culture that measures high on Hofstede's Power Distance scale (Hofstede, 1984).

Another reason that the two-hat model is preferred is that there is often an overlap between regions and the location of the national account headquarters. The eastern region manager could manage financial services and take a large New York bank as the national account. The central region manager may be based in Detroit and take a large automotive account. The western region manager could take a high-technology firm from Silicon Valley and be based in San Francisco. So there are a number of positives associated with the two-hat model.

There are some difficulties with the model as well. The obvious one is the overload on the regional managers. They may continue to manage their regions and give minimal attention to the national account. The leader's task is to prevent this imbalance. Second, the leadership group still may not become a team and may not work together effectively. Just because the regional managers are interdependent does not mean they will cooperate. If this model is used, then the selection criteria for regional managers should include collaborative skills. Third, the regional managers may not have the qualifications to manage both a region and a national account. Lack of experience is common when the customers are global accounts. Another issue is that the number of accounts and number of regions may be different. In the example, there are three regions and three national accounts. This situation is the ideal. Everyone wears two hats. But if there are five regions and three national accounts, the balance is broken. It is not impossible to function with this imbalance, but it puts a differentiating factor into the team, which will raise issues. The regional managers without national accounts will share neither the perspective nor the reciprocity of the others. The two-hat model works best when everyone wears two hats.

Examples of Two-Hat Structures

Our first example is a hybrid of the two-hat model that was used by many European corporations. We will look at Royal Dutch Shell's version of the hybrid. The second model is the one that was successfully used by Chrysler until the company was acquired by Daimler-Benz.

Royal Dutch Shell

European companies expanded internationally before U.S. companies did. The Europeans expanded when there was no World Trade Organization. It was a time of tariffs and protectionism. As a result, countries and regions were the main profit centers for these companies. Another distinguishing feature of companies whose home countries were Germany, Holland, and Switzerland was collective leadership. The CEO in many European companies was not as strong as a U.S. or U.K. CEO. The CEO was typically the chairman of the committee of managing directors. Each managing director on the committee wore two hats, a functional hat and a regional hat. The chairman did not have a region or a function. His power (and it always was a "he") was embodied in the role's neutrality to see the whole-company perspective. That is, each director had both a regional and functional perspective. But the chairman had no allegiance to any particular function or region. The Shell structure is shown in Figure 2.2.

Figure 2.2: Shell's Two-Hat Model

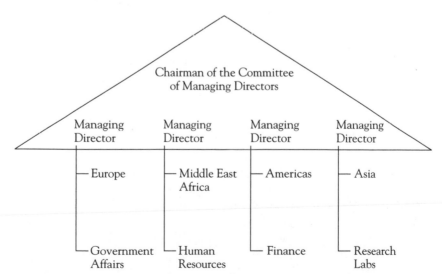

Reporting to each managing director (MD) is a function and a region. The directors represented these units in the committee of MDs. Each MD had the same set of responsibilities to aid in the cohesiveness of the committee. Collectively, they formed a leadership body to plan the future and oversee current performance.

As the world became characterized by deregulation and privatization and the WTO promoted a policy of free trade, businesses became more globally integrated. The response of many European companies was to add a business dimension to the organization. Each MD received a third hat, as shown in Figure 2.3. At Ciba-Geigy (now Novartis), the structure was referred to as the cube. All three dimensions were intended to be equal. As the world of business became more globally integrated, the business dimension became the most prominent. In Shell's case, the company adopted a structure very much like the Time Warner structure shown in Figure 1.1.

Figure 2.3: Shell's Three-Hat Model

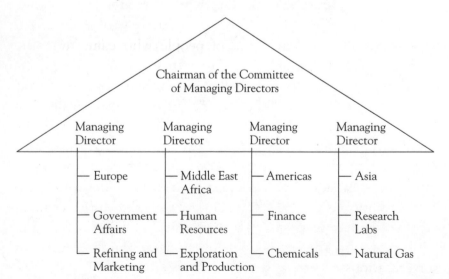

Chrysler

In the 1990s, Chrysler adopted a two-hat matrix structure. It was part of Chrysler's rebound and success leading up to the buyout by Daimler-Benz. Several points need to be made as a means of understanding the structure. First, all automobile manufacturers run the passenger car business as a single business through a functional organization structure. BMW, for example, runs its auto business through a global functional structure. The plant manager in South Carolina reports to the director of manufacturing in Munich.

Second, the auto industry was following a change path identical to that of the aerospace industry in the 1960s. The U.S. auto business was organized functionally and took five years or more to introduce a new car model. Then it was discovered that the Japanese introduced new models in two to three years. The reason was that the Japanese used strong product managers to lead the new car programs. In aerospace it was strong program managers who led the effort to get a man on the moon by 1970. So the auto industry adopted the model called "heavyweight product manager" because "matrix" was a dirty word at the time.

Third, Chrysler had some unique aspects of its own. The leadership was made up of people who came from the American Motors acquisition. From their "near-death experience," these leaders learned how to run a tight ship. As a result of the turnaround, they also formed a very cohesive leadership team. So when they formed their version of the heavyweight product manager, they created the two-hat model of the matrix structure, as shown in Figure 2.4. Each functional manager also had a product line responsibility. The product lines were called platforms. There was a platform for sport utility vehicles (SUVs) and vans, trucks, large cars, and small cars. The figure elaborates only the engineering function and the SUV platform organizations.

Figure 2.4: Chrysler's Two-Hat Matrix Structure

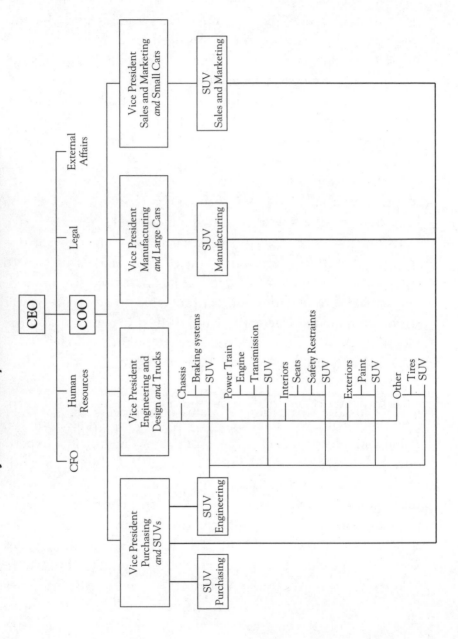

The structure of the engineering function (and also purchasing) follows from the structure of the automobile. The function is broken down into the chassis, power train, interiors, and exteriors. The power train is further subdivided into groups for the engine, transmission, drive shaft, and so forth. The chassis engineers are the experts in such areas as antilock braking systems and anti-rollover technologies. These are the advantages of a functional specialist structure. However, all these specialists must work together and combine their knowledge for a winning Chrysler minivan.

The role of the heavyweight product managers and their teams was to integrate the work of all the functional specialists into the realization of the holistic concept of a van, truck, or car. The platform manager for a new Chrysler minivan reported to the SUV product line head. In this case, the SUV head also runs purchasing. In each function, there is an SUV manager who reports to the function head and to the SUV platform head. These roles are identical to the subproject manager in aerospace. Then in each subunit there is an SUV head for chassis, power train, interiors, and exteriors. This structure is the matrix within a matrix to be explained in Chapter Four.

Another change that made the platform manager a heavyweight was the dedication of teams of engineers to the platform project and their colocation in the same building. Having people in the same building meant that design reviews could be held easily, face-to-face discussions happened naturally, and people could identify with the product. Even tier one suppliers moved their design teams into the new building in Auburn Hills. These changes transformed the groups into real teams and made the platform leaders real heavyweight product managers. Chrysler's performance in launching new products became much more effective and resulted in greatly compressed time frames.

The two-hat structure also resulted in a very effective leadership team. It was a common view in the industry that Chrysler had the most effective and cohesive management team. This effective management team was needed to set priorities and resolve conflicts that resulted from shared resources. Priorities needed to be established because each platform head wanted to launch a new product. Each platform head wanted the best engineers on his project. The leadership needed to match the new product portfolio with the resources available and assign the talent in the best way for Chrysler. This matching of priorities and resources took place continually and required a hands-on management team that was effective and decisive.

The Shell and Chrysler examples should bring to life the two-hat model of matrix organization. Chrysler is probably the best example of a company that used the model to run its business. At the time, the model caused a lot of conversation and questions. The cohesiveness of the leadership team had to be a major factor in the model's success. One of the causes of the many failures of matrix implementation was the lack of a strong, cohesive leadership team. References to the "warring tribes at Motorola" come to mind.

Summary

This chapter has described the two-hat model of matrix organization. It is useful for small companies or low-overhead operations, as a transition structure, and for use in authoritarian cultures. It is a demanding structure for the people wearing two hats. Although it promotes teamwork through reciprocity, it is more vulnerable to lack of teamwork. The model has been used both for transitions and for the continuous operation of companies. The next chapter discusses another variation on the matrix theme, the baton pass model.

3

THE BATON PASS MODEL

The baton pass model is another variation of matrix organization that companies have created to manage their unique challenges. In this case, managers recognized that during long product life cycles there are different management challenges at different stages of the cycle. Different leaders and teams are needed at these different stages. In a matrix, there is a need to pass the leadership baton between the different stages.

The first section of the chapter describes the concept using an example from the consumer goods industry. Then we explore the workings of the dual baton pass model used in the pharmaceutical industry.

The Consumer Goods Model

In the consumer goods industry, products or brands have long life cycles. Such products as Kleenex, Tide, and Colgate toothpaste have been around for a long time. However, they are continuously updated, improved, and relaunched. It is this cycle of revitalization and relaunch that leads to the baton pass model of matrix organization. The organization structure is shown in Figure 3.1. Instead of having the product side of the matrix report to the general manager, the product management role is split between the R&D and marketing functions. The responsibility for a product or brand is called a baton pass because the product manager in R&D starts first as the manager of both the product and the cross-functional team working on the products. When the development phase is near completion, the product manager from marketing joins the team and then takes

Figure 3.1: The Baton Pass Model

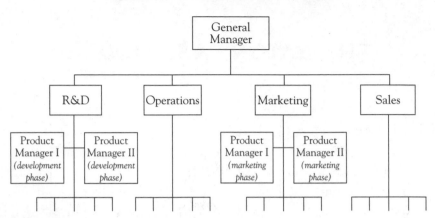

over the product management lead as the product is launched into distribution. The product management lead is the baton that gets passed between the product managers in the R&D and marketing functions. The members of the core team from the key functions remain on the team and provide the continuity during the leadership transition. The dynamics of the baton pass over the product's life cycle are shown in Figure 3.2.

After a few years, it is time to revitalize the product. At this time, the product management leadership shifts back to the R&D functions. More product and process R&D people are probably added to the effort. Then, as the new product nears relaunch, the marketing lead joins and then takes the leadership again. It is during this period of joint leadership that the product manager from R&D hands off to the product manager from marketing. As in a relay race, the baton pass is a critical change and requires practice and supervision until the product managers get it right.

To summarize, this model is used in product-focused businesses with long product life cycles. The initial development phase, where most of the work is R&D work, is led by a product manager from R&D. Once the product hits the market,

Figure 3.2: The Baton Pass Model in Action

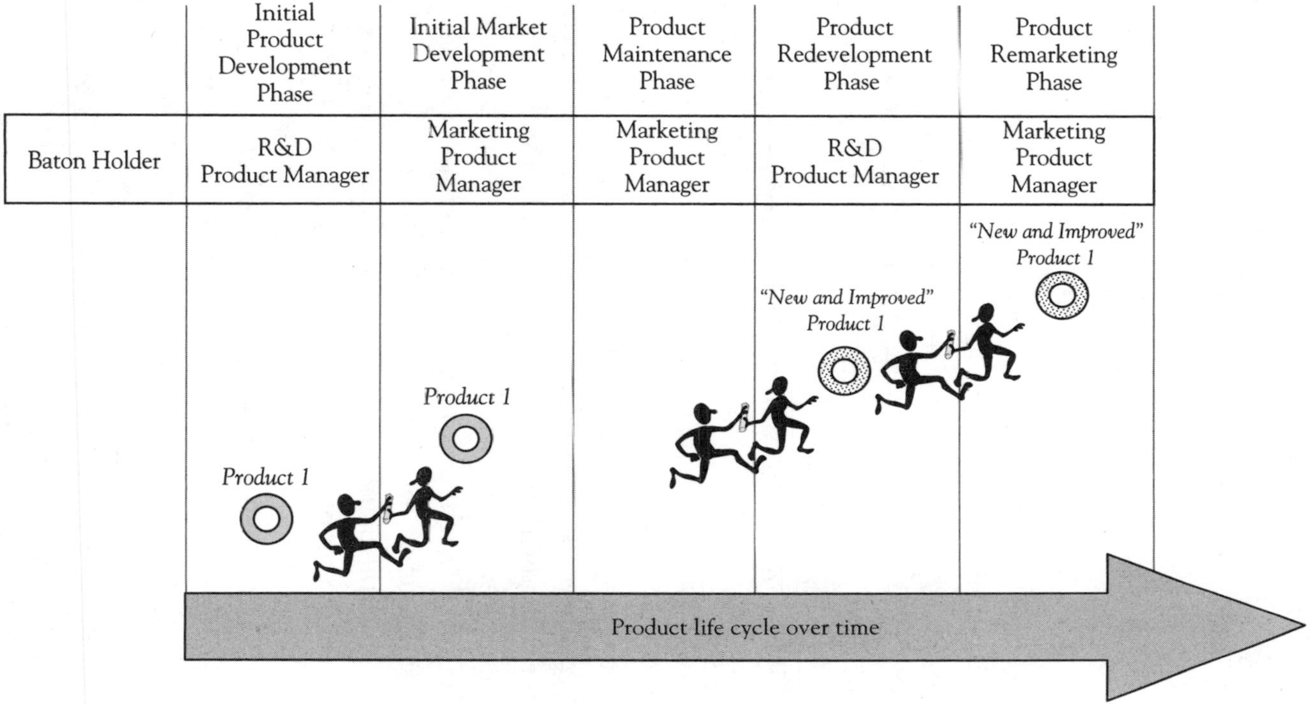

Baton Holder	Initial Product Development Phase	Initial Market Development Phase	Product Maintenance Phase	Product Redevelopment Phase	Product Remarketing Phase
	R&D Product Manager	Marketing Product Manager	Marketing Product Manager	R&D Product Manager	Marketing Product Manager

Product 1

Product 1

"New and Improved" Product 1

"New and Improved" Product 1

"New and Improved" Product 1

Product life cycle over time

management of that product entails making decisions about pricing, promotion, advertising, and product improvements that are mainly marketing tasks. As the work content shifts, the leadership shifts.

The Pharmaceutical Model

Another industry that uses the baton pass model is the pharmaceutical industry. Like consumer goods, it has long product development and life cycles. I briefly described the pharmaceutical industry's stagewise development of new products in Chapter One. The first phase is discovery, during which promising compounds are discovered. This is a phase of scientific discovery based on in-depth knowledge of such specialties as molecular biology, synthetic chemistry, biochemistry, and genetics, and of the new tools of combinatory chemistry and high-throughput screening. A promising compound results from these screening processes and tests in animals. The development phase is all about testing in humans. In terms of the new drug application (NDA) process, phase II and phase III are the human testing phases. Phase III comprises the large-scale clinical trials run by physicians with thousands of actual patients. When the NDA is approved by the Food and Drug Administration (FDA), the drug is launched into the markets of the world.

This third phase is referred to as "demand realization" at Eli Lilly. It is primarily a sales and marketing phase to generate and fulfill the demand for the drug. It is estimated that only 25 percent of the people who could benefit from a drug actually take the drug. Many people do not know that they have a treatable condition or may not go to a doctor. The doctor may not recognize the condition or may not prescribe the drug. So the product team's task is to deal with these demand realization issues. Then there are usually side effects. Some side effects are negative and may initiate some redesign of the product to eliminate them. Some side effects may be positive. For example, a tranquilizer may be effective on the central nervous system but may also reduce blood pressure. Either type of side effect may trigger more clinical trials, or what is called phase IV of the NDA.

There is a product manager and a team for the discovery phase, as described in Chapter One. In this chapter, I will describe the product managers and product teams in the development phase and the demand realization phase. There is a baton pass from the discovery phase team to the development phase team and then to the demand realization team. Because these companies receive patent protection, the life cycle of a compound may be ten to fifteen years.

We will use Eli Lilly as an example (Thomke, 1997; Wheelwright, 1999; and Malknight, 1999a, 1999b). The Lilly corporate organization structure is shown in Figure 3.3. Like other pharmaceutical companies, Lilly has a long tradition of being organized as a single-business functional organization and, like other companies, has slowly been organizing by therapeutic areas within the functions, such as discovery and marketing. Lilly was the first to organize by products and therapeutic areas at the corporate level. Figure 3.3 illustrates that there are the usual functions—science and technology, manufacturing, marketing—and geographic operations, which are mostly sales and local marketing. But there are also pharma product groups, such as skeletal products, neuroscience products, and diabetes care.

This increased focus on products and therapeutic areas reflected changes in the business environment. The time and cost for developing a new drug was escalating. In 1986, the estimated cost of developing a new drug was $125 million. In 2006, the cost was around $1 billion. Then there was the increasing prevalence of managed care. The product groups managed portfolios of products and looked more at the patient. The emphasis was as much on prevention and disease management as it was on treatment. The CEO could no longer be the single point of cross-functional integration. That was to become the role of the

Figure 3.3: Eli Lilly Corporate Structure

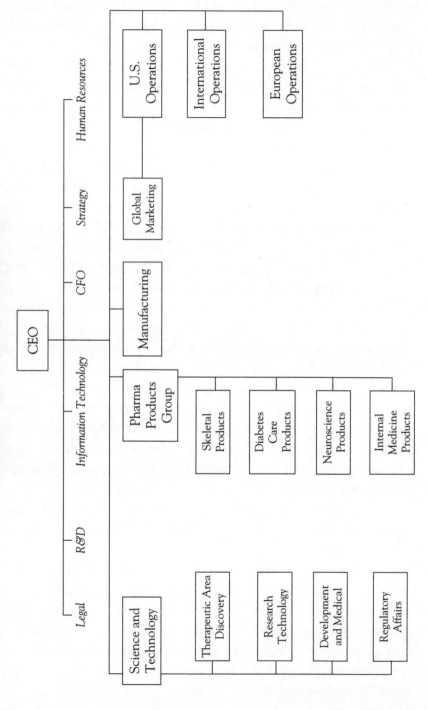

product teams and product groups. They had a time-to-market focus and controlled the P&L and budgets for their products.

The Development Phase

The development phase begins when the leadership committee reviews the evidence and authorizes a compound to enter into phase II testing. Phase II is testing of one hundred to three hundred humans who have the targeted disease and volunteer to participate. When this phase shows promise, phase III testing begins. These clinical trials take place in clinics and hospitals in about a dozen countries and involve several thousand volunteers who have the targeted condition. The trials are conducted by physicians who monitor the patients for safety, and observe and measure the compound's effectiveness. When the trials are completed and appear to have promise, the registration phase begins. An NDA is submitted to the FDA in the United States or similar regulatory bodies around the world. An NDA is typically around one hundred thousand pages. The approval process can take one or two years. When the drug is approved, the commercialization phase begins. The companies begin their commercialization planning during the approval phase.

Historically the development process was managed through the functional organizations. The functions focused on spreading the highly specialized people across projects so as to maximize their utilization. The project managers were low-level managers who often had more than one project. The project teams would meet monthly to review progress. The process took place sequentially as projects moved from one function to another. Not surprisingly, these projects were usually late. When the leadership inquired into project progress, it was impossible to determine accountability. Each function had done its job. As costs escalated and time delays ate into the patent protection time limit, the situation became unacceptable.

Around 1995, a new head of science and technology at Lilly decided to try something different. The new leader announced the implementation of two heavyweight product development teams to manage the development of the next two high-priority compounds (Clark and Wheelwright, 1995). Installing these new product development teams entailed several actions to increase the power base of the product teams. First, a core cross-functional team was created for each compound. Team members were dedicated full-time to the project. Each team was colocated. Second, a senior manager with a VP title was appointed as the full-time team leader. The team members reported to the VP for their day-to-day direction. Their long-term career development remained with their functions. Performance management was a joint product of the team leader and the function leaders. The team leader had two senior sponsors, one in science and technology and one in the pharma products group. The structure of the product teams is shown in Figure 3.4. The majority of the team members come from those functions shown in bold-face: regulatory affairs, medical, and development. Although the language of the change was couched in terms of heavyweight product teams, the change was to a product-function matrix organization.

A fourth change was that the product team would create an integrated product plan. The plan also articulated contracts to be filled by the functions. The work of all the functions was aligned to win approval of the FDA. The plan was also to address the customer needs of prescribing physicians and health care payers and to prepare for the commercialization phase. So the new team-driven way of bringing drugs to market represented a substantial change from the previous function-driven development process.

The change to a matrix structure, like any substantial change, caused some difficulties. People did not always understand why such a radical change was needed. Others who were not working on the teams were envious of the resources and attention

Figure 3.4: Development Phase Matrix Structure

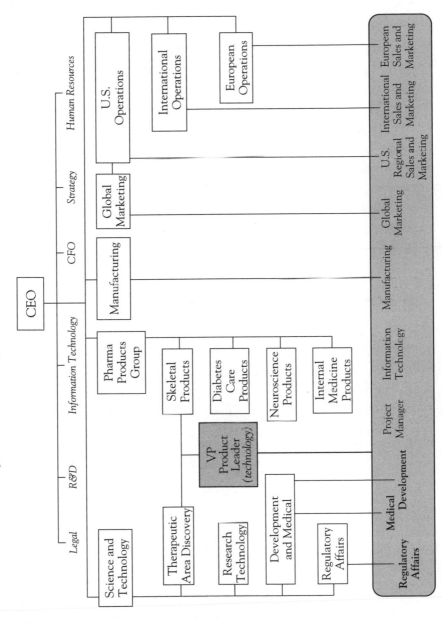

that the teams received. But in the end, the performance of the teams and the experience of the leadership team carried the day. The compounds were launched fifteen to eighteen months ahead of the original schedules, and the launches were much better planned. The decision was then taken to extend the heavy-weight team development process to all top-priority compounds. On average there are about ten teams in the development phase. The other decision was to keep the teams intact and extend them into the post-launch, or demand realization, phase.

In summary, the need for speed and focus on the products led to much stronger product managers and product teams, just as in the auto industry. This increase in power was accomplished by the introduction of product-function matrix organization in the development phase of the new product development process.

The Demand Realization Phase

Traditionally, following FDA approval, the technical, medical, and manufacturing staffs would return to their respective functions for their next assignments. The team would hand off the newly approved drug to sales and marketing for commercialization. The usual handoff problems occurred as new people had to get up to speed and the rich knowledge about the product was lost as the technical people returned to their labs. The technical people also failed to learn much about the marketplace, which reinforced the functional silos. Eli Lilly decided to extend the heavyweight product teams into the commercialization phase.

The teams maintained some of the people who worked on the product during the development phase. In addition to maintaining continuity, they picked up new indications for more clinical trials. For example, an osteoporosis drug also seemed to reduce the incidence of breast cancer. This observation led to more clinical trials to approve the drug for those new treatments. Such discoveries prolong the life of the drug and increase its revenues.

There are some differences between the commercialization and development phases. Although there are some technical issues, most of the challenges relate to commercializing the new drug. There are all the meetings to bring the countries into the launch process after approvals. There is the developing of marketing plans and conducting the ongoing market research. There is the transferring of knowledge and experience from early-launch countries to later-launch countries. There is the filling of supply lines for the launch countries. The product teams are active in all these launch activities. The staffing reflects the shift in activities. There are more sales and marketing people from the countries and fewer technical people. But, there is still the core, full-time, dedicated cross-functional team. Many members of the core team continue from the development team.

Another change to the team is a new leader. The leader in the development phase comes from the science and technology function. As shown in Figure 3.4, the role reports into the science and technology function as well as the pharma products group. The team leader for the demand realization phase comes from a sales or marketing background. He or she is a vice president but reports into the pharma products group. The structure is shown in Figure 3.5. In this case, the majority of the team members come from the various marketing functions (shown in boldface). The members of the team still report to the team leader and to their respective functions. There is an average of about thirty teams in total at Eli Lilly.

The product teams generate a cross-functional product life cycle plan. They identify where to invest to create the awareness for their product. There is the sales process of calling on the prescribing doctors. There are calls on health maintenance organizations and third-party payers. These organizations need to list the drug in the formularies in order to have patients get reimbursed for using it. There are investments in Web sites and

Figure 3.5: Demand Realization Phase Matrix Structure

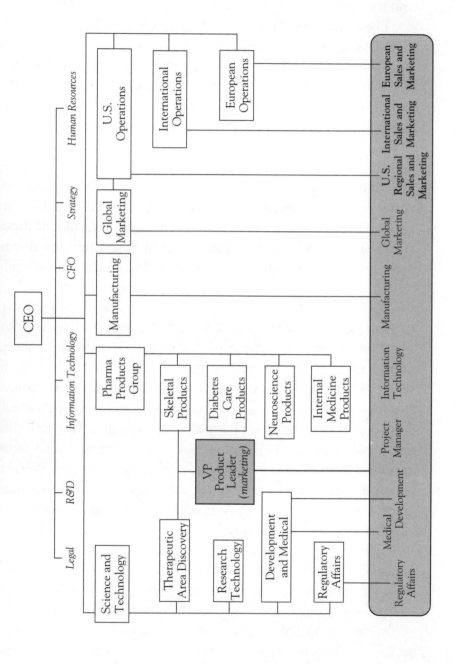

promotional materials. All these activities are aimed at demand realization over the product life cycle, which ends when it loses patent protection.

In summary, Eli Lilly has increased the power of product teams and team leaders by moving to a product-function matrix organization. The first teams, described in Chapter One, coordinate across specialists in the discovery research process to create potential new drugs. These drug candidates are then subjected to clinical trials in the development phase. A technical VP leads a full-time, dedicated cross-functional team to manage and fund the development process over three to five years. Some of the members of this team stay with the team into the demand realization phase. The baton is passed to a new VP from pharma products, who takes over and manages the team for the remainder of the products' patent protection.

Summary

This chapter has described the baton pass model of a matrix organization for the two-dimensional situation. It is a contrast to the simple two-dimensional and two-hat models. The baton pass model is appropriate for products with long life cycles. Because the business issues change over the cycle from technical to sales and marketing, the leadership is changed in a corresponding manner from technical to sales and marketing leaders.

The next chapter focuses on the design issues that arise when the matrix structure spans several levels. This situation is what we call the matrix within the matrix.

4

THE MATRIX WITHIN A MATRIX

It is common practice in most organizations today to find a matrix structure that spans three or four levels. We refer to this situation as the matrix within a matrix. It can present its own design challenges. It can also give a lot of people the same experience throughout the organization. The first part of the chapter defines the situation and discusses the design challenges. The next section gives another example that builds on the Time Warner example in Chapter One. A final example is taken from my experience with the Mars Pet Food Division.

Design Challenges of the Matrix Within a Matrix

The design of matrix structures often repeats itself at multiple levels of the organization. The design is usually a matrix within the matrix. There are three basic alternative designs. The first is the subproject manager design shown in Figure I.1 in the Introduction. A partial but more detailed structure is shown in Figure 4.1. Within the electronics specialty, we can see that some people are dedicated to projects I and II. They work directly for the subproject managers. Others work for the specialty A and B managers. These others may not be needed full-time on the projects or may move across both of them. Or the specialty people could be working on their own small electronics research projects. The matrix within a matrix means that the electronics director needs to be capable of running a small matrix within the electronics specialty.

This form of matrix, in which people work directly for the subproject manager and are dedicated to the project, is the ideal.

Figure 4.1: Matrix Within the Matrix

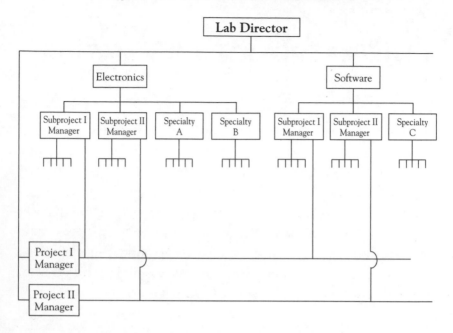

This model is possible where there are a few large projects that last six months or longer, as in the pharmaceutical industry examples. The subproject manager is a strong manager with many dedicated scientists. Other scientists move on and off the project as the subproject managers negotiate with the specialty managers for support. The director of electronics acts as tiebreaker, manages the team, and resolves disputes.

On other occasions, it is difficult if not impossible to organize a specialty or a function around projects or products. Then other options must be used. Operations is usually difficult to align by product. Let's look at the options for the operations function in a business unit. A subproduct role like the subproject role shown in Figure 4.1 is not possible. One option is to use the two-hat model for the people working for the director of operations. This option is shown in Figure 4.2. The structure shows the leader of manufacturing engineering and the plant

Figure 4.2: Two-Hat Model Within Operations

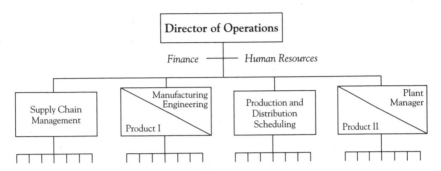

manager as wearing two hats. They run their function for all products and their product across all operations functions. They are the subproduct managers; they work for the director of operations and the product manager. If these two-hat managers are not capable of coordinating across all functions in operations—a likely situation—then another model is recommended.

The product-function matrix model is shown in Figure 4.3. There are two new managers added as subproduct managers I and II whose full-time job is coordinating across the operations functions to get their product to market and to see that orders are met and capacity is available. The difference between this model and the one shown in Figure 4.1 is that these subproduct managers have no one working directly for them. In this case, the members of their product teams wear two hats. On product I, the supply chain representative manages inventory in the supply chain function. The engineering representative manages the process control function as well as product I in the engineering function. The designer must weigh whether this complexity of organization is necessary. At the same time, these two-hat roles are good developmental experiences for middle managers. Because these subproduct managers do not have anyone working directly for them, it is harder for them to get things done than in the other two models. However, they are full-time coordinators and can devote all their time and energy

Figure 4.3: Product-Function Matrix Within Operations

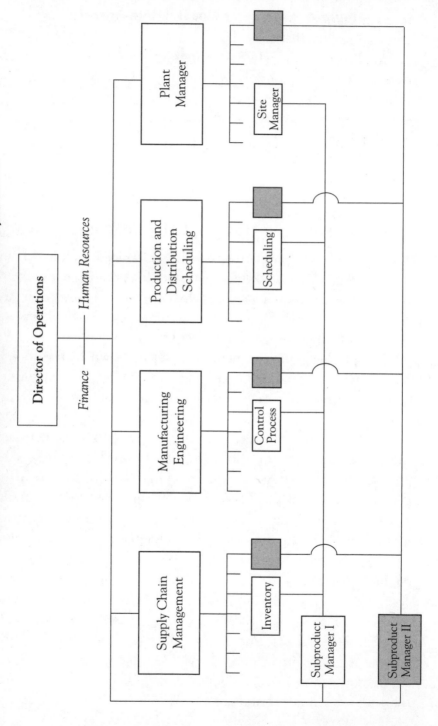

to coordination. And they report to the director of operations, who can resolve disputes.

In all three cases, the functional or specialty managers have to run a product-function or project specialty–function matrix in addition to managing their unit. Hence, a matrix within a matrix structure usually emerges. These managers will need additional skills as a result. But this small matrix provides a good developmental experience to test out replacements for the general manager.

Matrix Within a Matrix at the Corporate Level

In Chapter One I described the line-and-staff model, which is now referred to as the function–profit center matrix. I used the example of Time Warner (TW) to illustrate a holding company version of the matrix. We can use it again to illustrate the matrix within a matrix, as shown in Figure 4.4.

Figure 4.4: Matrix Within a Matrix at Time Warner

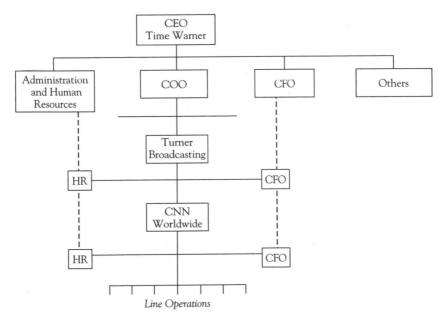

The CEO has an HR function and a CFO reporting to him. The president of Turner Broadcasting and the other businesses also have an HR and a CFO function reporting to them. These business functions also report to their corporate functional bosses, as shown in the matrix in Chapter One (Figure 1.1). The same pattern replicates itself within the Turner Broadcasting business. The CNN Worldwide president also has an HR and a CFO function. So these patterns can repeat themselves for many levels in large organizations.

Managers constantly question if all these levels of staff are really needed. But what usually happens is that P&L managers believe that they need their staffs but question if others really need their staffs. Companies have found several ways of dealing with the controversy. First, not all functions are replicated. For example, the strategy function may not be replicated at every level, but may be combined with the CFO role. The HR and CFO roles are the ones that usually appear at most levels. Second, some levels may share a function. For example, the COO role does not have a CFO role dedicated to it. The COO usually shares the CFO with the CEO. There may be a controller that is dedicated to the COO, however. Sharing across levels is not as common as sharing at the same level. For example, the president of CNN Worldwide may share a CFO with the president of CNN Domestic. So there are some ways to simplify and economize rather than blindly replicating the pattern throughout the structure.

Mars Pet Food Example

A few years ago, I worked with the Mars pet food division on implementing a matrix organization. Like all of Mars' divisions, pet foods was organized functionally. And like all functional organizations, the division was struggling when introducing new products across functions and prioritizing for several product lines. At the time, the pet foods division was standardizing on two global brands. It had adopted Pedigree for dog food and Whiskas for cat food. It also wanted to improve on new product launches when rebranding and relaunching all the current products.

Pet foods adopted the matrix structure and the baton pass variation. Both marketing and product development had strong managers who oversaw the dog and cat food categories with their functions. They took the lead in managing the dog and cat category teams. The other functions posed some problems, as we can see in Figure 4.5.

Procurement was organized by commodities, which went into both dog and cat foods. Operations was organized by manufacturing sites, supply chain, and process technology, which also served both the dog and cat food categories. Sales and distribution was organized by regions and customer. So from a product viewpoint, one could not get a clear line of sight through these functions. There were several interfaces and several different types of interfaces in each function.

The pet foods division took different approaches to creating a single interface in each function. In sales and distribution, the leadership created a product function. These product specialists would assist the account managers in the field when in-depth product knowledge was needed in the sales process. They would also be the sales and distribution representatives on the dog and cat category teams. This design means that the sales and distribution (S&D) manager had to run an S&D matrix within the pet foods divisional matrix.

In procurement and operations, pet foods chose to go with the two-hat model. The leader of the fish commodity department took a position on the cat food category team. Most of the fish purchases went into cat food. The meat commodity department head sat on the dog food category team. In this case, most of the meat purchases went into dog food. In operations, the two strongest leaders were the manufacturing and supply chain managers. They decided among themselves to have the supply chain

Figure 4.5: Mars Pet Food Structure

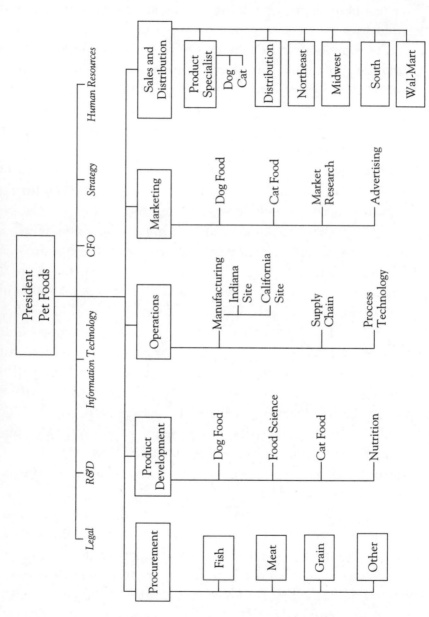

head sit on the cat food category team, and the manufacturing manager took the position on the dog food category team. Both the procurement and operations heads must also run a functional matrix with the pet foods divisional matrix.

The implementation went well in operations and in S&D. The procurement manager ran into problems. He was a command-and-control type. He did not like the category team leaders influencing "his people." He became a bottleneck when he insisted that all contacts go through him. Further, he did not coordinate well within the function. He had a one-on-one style. In the matrix, he needed to get the people around a table and coordinate the product launch needs across the commodities. The addition of categories made the people more interdependent, and required teamwork on new products. The procurement head was transferred to the confectionery division in exchange for another manager who could lead teams more effectively.

The pet foods division president ran the top group as a team. The rebranding and relaunching of products was difficult but successful. The success was attributable to the president's ability to run a category-function matrix at the division level, and to the functional leaders' ability to run a matrix within a matrix within their functions.

Summary

This chapter reviewed the issues that arise when a matrix structure spans several levels of the total structure. The two-hat model arises often in this context of a matrix within a matrix. The functions cannot always easily line up with product, project, or customer teams. The two-hat model creates a single interface, but requires that a matrix be led at multiple levels.

5

BALANCING POWER AND DEFINING ROLES

One of the key attributes of a matrix organization is the relative balance of power across the different sides of the structure. One of the leaders' tasks is to maintain a distribution of power across the matrix in line with the demands of the strategy. In this chapter, I describe the levers that leaders can use to change the power distribution. One of the levers is the change of decision rights or responsibilities. The definition of roles and responsibilities is also a key requirement of the implementation of a matrix. The last section of the chapter presents responsibility charts as a tool that can be used to shift power and clarify roles.

Designing Power Bases

As I've stated, a key feature of matrix structures is the relative balance of power between the two sides of the matrix. In a pure functional structure, all the power is in the functions. In a pure product structure, all the power is in the product units. When a company's strategy requires both functional excellence and fast time to market, the structure needs to balance the power of the managers who fill the functional and product roles. In this section, we identify the levers that leaders can use to balance the power distribution as required by the strategy.

Discussions about matrix often assume that the two sides of the matrix are of equal power. That situation is possible, but more often than not there is an imbalance of power and authority between the two sides. That imbalance is appropriate if it derives from the firm's strategy. Let us use the multinational matrix of countries and business units to illustrate how organization designers can fine-tune the power balance.

Most multinationals built their global businesses country by country. Initially the profit centers were countries and regions. But as cross-border trade and transfers of technology have increased, the power of units with cross-border coordination responsibilities has increased. These cross-border units are usually the global business units. The power distribution change is illustrated in Figure 5.1. In the 1970s and 1980s, such companies as Philips, 3M, and Colgate Palmolive all were organized as geography-dominant matrix organizations, as shown in Figure 5.1 (A). Today, food companies like Nestlé and Kraft are still organized in this "business lite" structure. But Philips is now organized in a structure like the one illustrated in Figure 5.1 (C). How is this shift in power accomplished? We look at some possible methods in the next sections.

Structure

The most straightforward method of shifting power to a unit is to report that unit higher in the hierarchy. A company's organization chart is actually a display of its intended strategic priorities. For example, up until the late 1990s, business units at Procter & Gamble reported to regional managers in North America and Europe, who reported to the CEO. In their Organization 2005 initiative, P&G created global business units and geographic market development organizations and reported both to the CEO. This change shifted more power to the business side of the matrix. Today P&G's structure is close to the one shown in Figure 5.1 (B) as a balanced matrix.

Staffing

In combination with the level of reporting, the quality of the person placed in the role will increase or decrease the perceived

Figure 5.1: Power Distribution Continuum Across the Geography-Business Matrix

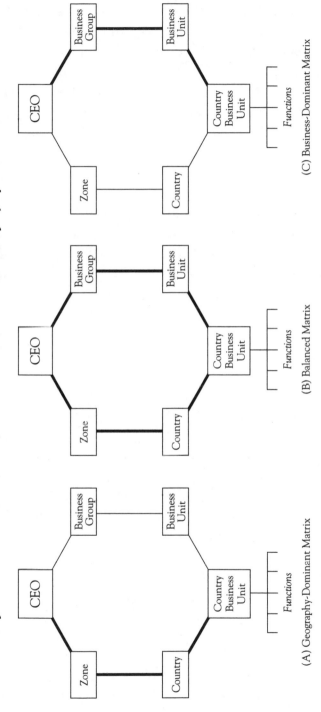

(A) Geography-Dominant Matrix

(B) Balanced Matrix

(C) Business-Dominant Matrix

power of the role. So even if the role has no formal authority, the status and reputation of the person will give him or her a great deal of personal power. This personal power is magnified if the individual is also skilled at influencing without authority. Through this kind of talent selection, the organization designer can fine-tune the power distribution to match what is called for by the strategy.

Information Systems

The global business managers increase in power when they have accounting and information systems to support their businesses. When they have visibility into global and country inventories, they can initiate supply chain programs. When the accounting systems are in place, they often reveal that a business is losing money in a country. If there are no global P&L accounts for a business, it is a situation of the business manager's opinion versus the country manager's opinion. Facts and data increase the power base of the global managers. They can legitimately initiate actions in countries that are losing money.

It is also very important that both sides of the matrix use the same information. Often the business side creates a new cross-border information system so that it can compare common figures for inventory, depreciation, and so on. However, if country managers are not part of the process and continue to use their old systems, a new set of disputes will arise. When the numbers for something like inventory do not match, the argument turns to who has the best numbers. To avoid these time-wasting disputes, everyone should use the same information. If the creation of a new system will take years, the company should create a "quick-and-dirty" temporary one. It is more important at this stage that everyone use the same information than it is to have the best information.

These accounting systems are useful when dealing with the global customer. Often the costs and revenues are not balanced by country. For example, an HP sales team worked for several years to sell a computer-aided design system to Siemens. When Siemens accepted HP's proposal, the first system was installed in Siemens' U.K. subsidiary, and the second one in the subsidiary in Thailand. Thus all of HP's costs of selling were incurred in Germany, whereas the revenues were booked in the United Kingdom and Thailand. A global accounting system allows the global account team in Munich to get credit for revenues as well as costs. As I mentioned earlier, it is also important that everyone use the same information, otherwise games are played as to whose information is correct. Multidimensional organizations require multidimensional information systems.

Voice in the Planning Process

Once a company has country and business P&L accounting systems, the next step is to use that information in the planning and budgeting process. The global business manager can then have a voice in the goal-setting process. So even in a business lite matrix, the global business managers can influence the profit, growth, and market share goals of their businesses in Germany and Japan.

I still remember a statement made to me by a product manager from the computer industry. He said "I don't care whether the salespeople work for me or not, just so long as I get to set their quota." Because the quotas drive the behavior of salespeople, having a voice in the quota-setting process was seen as more powerful than having authority over the salespeople. Of course managers get this voice only if the leadership opens the discussion process and listens to the business side of the matrix. As we will see, leaders' behavior makes a big difference in a matrix.

Rewards Distributed on the Basis of Goals

Once the business goals for a country are set, they have to mean something. It is possible for a country to exceed its profit targets by doing very well in a few businesses while doing poorly in the new, small-growth businesses. Matrix organizations run best when countries are required to meet all their business goals. The countries hate this additional complexity, but it is the only or the best way to give emphasis to the new and the small business. So the reward system puts some teeth into the goal-setting process by requiring country managers to meet all goals to which they have committed.

Decision Authority

The global business manager may get specific decision rights. For example, in the age of the global customer, the global business manager may be given the authority to make pricing policy decisions. The problem is that if country managers reduce the price of a product for a global customer in their country, the global customer will ask for that same price on that same product in all countries. As a result, price changes usually need the approval of the global business manager to prevent the reduction of global margins without a good reason. Later we will explore the use of responsibility charts to clarify decision rights as well as to shift decision authority.

Budgets

Another method of giving the global business manager more power is to give him or her a budget for particular activities. Global businesses very often take responsibility for global product development. They are then given a budget for R&D. The countries can propose projects for funding from the global business unit. Changes to the funded R&D projects would require approval from the global business manager. In this way, the global business dimension of the matrix acquires specific powers for specific activities. Giving the budget to heavyweight product managers was one of the ways that Eli Lilly shifted more power to the product lines.

These changes to the power distribution we've looked at so far are accomplished by using methods associated with the policy areas of the Star Model (see Figure I.4). By working through the Star Model and using staffing, goal setting, information systems, reward systems, and roles and responsibilities, the organization designer can fine-tune the power distribution across the matrix.

Dual Authority

The final step to creating a power balance is to include the global business manager in the performance appraisal of the country business unit manager. That is, the business unit contained in the country would report to the global business unit and to the country. The country manager and the global business unit manager would jointly select the country business unit manager, jointly agree on the business goals in the country, and jointly assess the manager's performance. This change creates the dual-authority system and the two-boss situation. It arises when a power balance is desired. However, the country manager and the global business manager have different responsibilities and authority over different activities. These roles are established using responsibility charts, as discussed in the next section.

In this way, the organization designer can shift power across the dimensions of the matrix. The dual authority creates a power balance that is shown in Figure 5.1 (B). The shift from the balanced position to the business-dominant and "geography lite" position shown in Figure 5.1 (C) can be accomplished by removing the dual authority from the country manager. Any of the other tools, such as information systems and budgets, can be removed. The enhancing of the power position of the global business and the diminishing of the geography is what took place in the 1990s. Many companies, such as Philips and BP, now have global structures like the one shown in Figure 5.1 (C).

Roles and Responsibilities

Matrix organizations are often accused of being ill defined, with fuzzy interfaces and unclear roles. This situation need not arise. The designer instead can be very clear about roles and interfaces. That is the purpose of the responsibility chart, in addition to balancing power. The process of defining roles and responsibilities begins after the structure has been designed and the people are in their new roles. After any change to the organization, each employee will want to know "What is my role?" Whether working with matrix structures inside the company or executing alliances across partner companies, the question is always "Who is responsible for what?" One of the most useful tools in implementing any organization design, and particularly matrix designs, is the responsibility chart, an example of which is shown in Figure 5.2.

Figure 5.2: Example of a Responsibility Chart

Roles / Decisions	Sales	Segment marketing	Insurance	Mutual funds	Marketing council	CEO	Finance	Human resources	Regional team
Product price									
Package design									
Package price									
Forecast	A	R	C	C	C	I	I	X	X
Product design									

Note: For clarity, only one line of the matrix has been completed.

The structure determines which roles need definition. It is best to stick to only two levels of structure for this exercise. As shown in the chart, the roles form the (vertical) columns. The key decisions that these roles will execute form the (horizontal) rows. These decisions are the ones that are likely to be contentious. They are the ones around which the turf and territory issues are likely to surface.

To fill in the chart, the people who play the roles listed in the columns are interviewed by a neutral person. The role players suggest which decisions should be listed. It is best to list about twenty to thirty decisions. Too few decisions will not provide the clarity needed to know who is responsible for what. Too many will require a laborious effort to define the roles; it will seem too bureaucratic.

After the chart is completed, the people playing the roles fill out the chart individually. They answer the question, "How should we make decisions in the new organization?" To complete the chart, they need a code to describe the different ways that a role can affect a decision. Four is the usual number, with "no formal role" a fifth option:

R = Responsible
A = Approve
C = Consult
I = Inform
X = No Formal Role

The person who is responsible for making a decision is given an R in the appropriate box. The segment marketing group, for example, is responsible for the forecast. That is, the segment marketing people initiate the process, collect the information, maintain the database for it, and arrive at a forecast.

Ideally, there would be one R for each row and no entries of any other kind. However, in matrix organizations, other types of roles are at play in joint decisions. For example, the sales function does not do the forecast but must approve it. That is, sales must concur with the forecast before segment marketing can implement it. Therefore, sales's box gets an A. If there is no agreement, segment marketing and sales must negotiate. Again, sales cannot overturn the forecast, but must agree with it. If there is still no agreement, the issue is raised to the CEO for resolution. Others may not be required to approve a decision, but they must be consulted by the responsible party. The C is placed in the box for the general managers of the insurance and mutual funds businesses, as well as the marketing council. This signifies that segment marketing must get input from all of them before making a commitment. However, once having gotten their input, segment marketing can decide what to do; it does not need their agreement. It only needs to consult with the parties who have been given C's.

Finally, some roles do not need to be involved in a decision before it is made, but do need to know the outcome afterward. For example, the finance function needs to know the forecast so that it can make cash forecasts and so on. But finance does not need to participate in the forecast itself. Finance needs to be informed, so it is given an I in the appropriate box. Others have no formal role in this decision. If those given an R want to involve them, that is fine. These people receive an X.

After each role occupant has completed the chart, everyone meets, usually off-site, for a half day or a full day to discuss and reach agreement on the role assignments. Usually the results of the individual chart assessment are displayed. There is almost always complete disagreement. The disparity motivates a lively discussion. A facilitator then proceeds, decision by decision. For each decision, the discussion revolves around why a person should participate. What value does that person provide? Is it worth the complexity and possible time delay? This discussion is the real value of the exercise. People begin to talk about how they will work together. They teach one another about their roles. In the end, there is usually consensus and a completed chart. If there is no consensus, then the CEO must say, "Okay, I have heard the arguments. Most people prefer this way. Let's try it and see if it works. We'll review the outcomes in three months. Next decision."

In either case, in the end the chart is completed. To define a role, one simply proceeds down the column under the role title. The entries become the assignments. The process educates the participants and creates consensus about roles and responsibilities. The chart provides the clarity needed in the flexible, ever-changing organizations of today. If another change is made to the organization, the chart is simply redrawn. It is a tool that can be used frequently and disseminated throughout the organization as needed.

Summary

In this chapter, we discussed the power levers that leaders can use to change the power base of managers on their leadership teams. These levers are the leaders' tools to align the power requirements of the team with the power demands in the business environment. We also looked at responsibility charts. These charts can be used both to align power balances and to define roles and responsibilities in the matrix.

Part Two

COMPLEX MATRIX STRUCTURES

One of the reasons that matrix organizations have been so difficult to master is that companies have kept applying them to more and more complex situations. The original two-dimensional matrix structures that were implemented in aerospace and R&D labs were standard practice by the 1990s. A similar product manager–functional specialist model was applied to the new product development process in business units in manufacturing companies. This matrix also became standard practice by the 1990s. So certainly by 2000, the simple two-dimensional matrix that we discussed in Part One was mastered by most competent companies. To be sure, these companies still struggle to modify and improve their matrix organizations—when integrating acquisitions, for example. But today, implementing the two-dimensional matrix in top companies is a solved problem.

The difficulty now is in mastering the three-, four-, or other multidimensional matrix organization. So even if a manufacturing firm has mastered the matrix in its R&D labs and business units, it experiences a new challenge when implementing a matrix of business units and countries. The international expansions of many companies present them with the challenge of coordinating businesses, countries, and functions in a three-dimensional matrix. I discuss this form of matrix in Chapter Six and describe the variations in organizations that have been developed by both service and manufacturing companies.

In the 1990s, companies added a fourth dimension to their structures. This fourth dimension was usually a customer dimension. That is, as companies expanded internationally, they wanted the same suppliers and same levels of service in all countries in which they were present. The suppliers needed to add a customer dimension to their country, business unit, and functional structures.

A new hybrid structure emerged in these four-dimensional organizations. These hybrids were called front-back structures. The front end was a customer-facing unit that was organized by geography, customer segments, or both. The back end was organized around business units and large-scale functions. The purpose of this hybrid was to achieve customer responsiveness in the front and global scale in the back.

The organizational challenge is to link the front and back together. It is in this linkage that matrix plays an important role. We look at this front-back hybrid structure in Chapter Seven.

IBM has become one of the most complex organizations in the world, if not the most complex. In Chapter Eight, I describe the IBM structure, which has at least six organizational dimensions. It has the standard business unit, geography, function, and customer four-dimensional front-back model. But it has added units for solutions and channels to the structure. IBM is a perfect example of how good companies continually add new dimensions to their matrix organizations. These companies are therefore continually challenged to integrate and coordinate the new dimensions with their existing multidimensional matrix organizations. Thus one of the reasons that matrix organization seems to be an overly difficult type to manage is that good companies continuously escalate the complexity to be managed. Having mastered the two-dimensional matrix, companies move to three-, four-, or, in IBM's case, six-dimensional structures. By mastering more dimensions, companies can create more value for their customers. They can master more complexity and get a "leg up" on their competitors. Mastering complexity is a hard advantage to copy.

The IBM example always raises issues. The first is "How do you manage all this complexity?" This issue is addressed in Part Three. Briefly, complexity is managed by selecting and developing people who can execute the management processes that align objectives and by rewarding both achievement and collaboration. The second issue is, "Is there a limit to the complexity that can be managed successfully?" And third, if there is a limit, "What is it?" I think that there has to be a limit, but every time that I think we are at the limit, a company like IBM adds another dimension. So we have to stay tuned for the next episode to see if and when there is a limit.

6

THE THREE-DIMENSIONAL MATRIX

As stated in the introduction to this part of the book, most companies have mastered the two-dimensional matrix. Certainly the corporate function–business unit matrix is standard practice in business today. To be sure, some companies are better at matrix than others. And all companies have some problems and need to make changes and improvements. But the focus today is on implementing three- and four-dimensional matrix structures. In this chapter, we focus on the three-dimensional structure. For most companies, the three-dimensional matrix is a consequence of doing business internationally.

In this chapter, we expand on the international business unit matrix introduced in Chapter Five and shown in Figure 5.1. We then add the functions to that two-dimensional design. When choosing between the three types of structure shown in Figure 5.1, we follow the Star Model. That is, different strategies will require different structures. So we begin the chapter with a discussion of the different international strategies and how they affect structures. Then we will examine the geography-dominant model, the balanced matrix, and finally the business-dominant model. The last section gives some other examples of three-dimensional matrix designs.

International Strategy

The three models for managing a country–business unit matrix were presented in Chapter Five. In this section, we identify the criteria for choosing which model is best for you at this time. Then we add the third or functional dimension.

The key strategic factors in guiding the choice of international matrix forms are (1) the amount of cross-border coordination, (2) the activity level of host governments in the economic process, and (3) the level of diversification of the international portfolio.

Cross-Border Coordination

Cross-border coordination is the first factor that impacts the distribution of power and authority between the countries and the businesses. In general, when there is a high level of cross-border coordination, the power goes to those roles responsible for the coordination—that is, to business unit and functional managers. When most coordination takes place within borders, the power rests with the country and regional managers. There are several factors that impact the amount of cross-border coordination.

Level of Fixed Costs High-fixed-cost strategies directly impact the amount of cross-border coordination. Companies cannot afford to duplicate the fixed-cost investments in every country in which they are present. They therefore invest in a few countries and supply the rest with cross-border transfers of products, services, and technology. Business units and functions hold the decision-making power in high-fixed-cost industries, such as chemicals, semiconductors, and pharmaceuticals. These fixed-cost investments can take several forms.

High fixed costs result from large investments in capital assets, such as factories and data centers. Companies that invest billions in chemical plants, semiconductor fabrication plants, and liquid crystal display factories are good examples. Companies in these industries must invest in only a few countries and supply the rest with products. The responsibility for supply rests with business units, operations functions, and supply chain functions. So in capital-intensive industries, the decision-making power rests with managers in these roles.

Companies following R&D-intensive strategies also incur high fixed costs. These companies invest in new product development in a few countries and transfer the products around the world. The transfer is managed by business unit and R&D managers. So when companies spend more than 5 percent of sales in R&D, power shifts to the businesses and to the R&D function.

Global brands and heavy investment in advertising and promotion through a single ad agency shift power away from countries. Again it is the business unit heads and in this case the chief marketing officer who become more influential.

Products and Markets Standard products and homogeneous markets facilitate cross-border transfers of products and services and reduce the power of country managers. The business units and supply chain functions acquire more responsibility and authority. Alternatively, when markets are heterogeneous and products are unique to countries and regions, it is the country managers who can best coordinate the business.

Semiconductors are again a good example of global products; Intel's Centrino is used in laptops across the world. Thus semiconductor companies are dominated by global business managers. White goods, such as refrigerators, vary in size around the world. Europeans like front-loading laundry equipment; Americans like top-loading washers and dryers. So white goods businesses are run through region-dominant matrix structures.

Customers and Competitors When the key customers and the toughest competitors are local, the country managers are in the best position to manage the business. When they are global, the business units and global account manager are in the best position to make decisions. When faced with a mix of local, regional, and global customers and competitors, a power balance and an allocation of responsibilities work best.

Sometimes a company chooses a specific customer strategy. Citibank's commercial and investment banking business chose to supply global products to global customers. It had an advantage at the global level. At the local level, serving local customers, Citibank was just another bank. Its matrix shifted from a country-dominant structure to a customer segment–dominant and global product–dominant structure.

Transportability Cross-border coordination takes place when a product or service can be created in one place and sold in another. This transportability occurs when the product has a high value relative to its transport costs. Semiconductors are shipped across borders because they are standard products and because they have high value and low transport costs. Cement is a fairly standard product too, but has a low ratio of value to transport costs. A cement plant is not competitive outside of a radius of about 150 miles.

Service businesses have traditionally been local businesses, with the service produced and consumed at the same site. Some services—such as hotels, restaurants, and construction—are likely to remain local; others are becoming more transportable because of telecommunications advances and will become still more transportable with the Internet. Until now, retailing, banking, education, and health care all required the customer to go to the store, branch, hospital, or school; these businesses were structured around regional profit centers. But with home shopping, home banking, distance learning, and remote medicine, these industries and their organizations are changing. When services are transportable, business units, which are focused on market segments or product lines, become the dominant profit center and principal axis of the matrix. The more transportable a product or service, the more the customer will be supplied across borders; the more cross-border supply that takes place, the more that strategies must be formulated—and distribution coordinated—on a cross-border basis.

In summary, the business units and functions will be the dominant axis of the matrix when there is a high level of cross-border coordination. A high level of cross-border coordination occurs in businesses with high fixed costs, standard products, homogeneous markets, global customers and competitors, or a high ratio of value to transport costs. The country or geographic dimension will be dominant when there are low fixed costs, unique products, heterogeneous markets, local customers, local competitors, or a low ratio of value to transport costs. Most companies are going to have a mix of these strategic factors. They will need to be both global and local, and hence the use of the matrix. Depending on the priorities of the factors, these matrix structures will be either geography dominant, balanced, or business dominant.

Active Host Governments and Institutions

A second strategic factor is the degree to which the government participates in a country's economic process (Doz, 1988). The government may be a customer, a partner, a regulator, or some combination of the three. When the government is active and demanding, the company needs a strong country manager to maintain a relationship and negotiate with the appropriate governmental units. When a company needs a strong country manager *and* cross-border coordination requires a strong business unit manager, the matrix organization is appropriate.

Royal Dutch Shell is a good example. Shell has moved away from its matrix organization by increasing the decision-making power of the business units. However, a strong country manager—and the matrix—are still maintained in places like Malaysia, where oil is a strategic industry managed by a state-owned oil company that is simultaneously the regulator of the industry, a partner, and a competitor. In Malaysia, Petronas competes in the upstream exploration and production business as well as in the downstream refining and marketing business. A strong local Malay is the chairman and country manager of Shell

Malaysia; his task is to balance the multifaceted relationship between the businesses, the state-owned oil company, and the Malaysian government in the best interests of Shell. Similar situations arise in other Asian countries, most of which follow the Japanese model of government-guided economies. In many of these countries, personal connections (*guanxi*) are more important than a company's quality program in gaining market access; having a country manager with connections and power is requisite.

There will always be some form of country manager as long as there are country governments, unions, and other institutions. The more active, powerful, and demanding these local institutions, the stronger the country manager must be to represent the company and negotiate on its behalf.

Host governments can limit cross-border strategies in numerous ways. They can require exports, local value-added, local suppliers, partners, or product certification; they can limit imports, profit repatriation, access to foreign exchange, and so on as well. They can also provide incentives, such as subsidies, tax forgiveness, and privileged access to markets or resources. All these limits and incentives are usually negotiable. The country is looking for jobs, industrial activity in depressed areas, promotion of some ethnic groups, and, most of all, modern technology; the company is looking for market access. Countries with large, attractive markets—China, India, and Indonesia, for example—use their bargaining power to extract technology in return for market access.

The trend in the 1990s had been to reduce the strength of national governments in the economic process—free-trade agreements, global capital markets, deregulation, and privatization were shifting the power from national governments to markets. This trend resulted in increased cross-border trade, with stronger business unit managers to coordinate it. Since the turn of the century, these forces have been muted by a rise in protectionism and active host governments in the growth countries, such as Brazil, China, Russia, and India. These changes in the business environment have brought a return to power of the country manager. One of the values of the matrix organization is its more flexible capability to fine-tune the distribution of power and authority. This capability is discussed in more detail in Chapter Thirteen.

Diversity of the International Business Portfolio

Diversity is measured by the number of different businesses in the portfolio, especially the differences in business logic (Galbraith, Lawler, and Associates,1993, chap. 2). For example, ethical and over-the-counter (OTC) drugs are both pharmaceutical businesses, but they differ in their fundamental logics. The OTC business is marketing-driven, with heavy expenses in advertising and promotion; the ethical pharmaceuticals firm is an R&D business, with expenses going mostly to discovering and developing new compounds. When portfolios have several different business logics in them, coordination across the business units is difficult to achieve; in general, the greater the diversity of the international portfolio, the stronger the business unit manager and the weaker the geographic manager. With a diverse portfolio, it is easier for a business manager to coordinate across borders within a business than for a geographic manager to coordinate across diverse businesses within a border.

The strategic factor of interest is the diversity of the *international* portfolio; a company's international organization is influenced by the diversity of its international portfolio, not its domestic portfolio. Often a company is diverse in its home country, but takes businesses international only when it has an advantage. Toyota, for example, is more diverse in Japan, where it is involved in the construction and mobile phone businesses, than it is abroad, where it is superior only in cars and trucks.

The diversity of the international portfolio can take a range of forms, from the related portfolio, like that of P&G, to the holding company portfolio, like that of Time Warner. Nestlé is an example of a company following a related diversification strategy: it has multiple products in multiple businesses, but operates with a single business logic. Nestlé has thousands of products and brands in the food and beverage businesses, all consumer packaged goods. They are marketing and distribution businesses that have a common customer—the mass merchandiser—and are driven by a system of brand management. When Nestlé diversified into bottled waters, it had to learn a new business, but not a new way of doing business. Not surprisingly, Nestlé builds its profit centers around country managers; the marketing-oriented country manager comprehends the business range and coordinates businesses by going through shared distribution channels to a common customer.

The other extreme is the conglomerate. This multibusiness entity has a portfolio of highly unrelated businesses and makes no attempt to coordinate them. Time Warner and United Technologies run their businesses through global business managers. There are some country and regional managers, but they run with a business-dominant model.

Table 6.1 summarizes our strategy discussion. When the factors in the middle column of the table are high priority, the company chooses a geography-dominant matrix. When the factors on the right side are salient, the company chooses a business-dominant matrix. When they are of equal importance, a balanced matrix is chosen. Let us look at each of these models.

The Geography-Dominant Matrix

We have been using Nestlé as our example; let us examine more closely the Nestlé structure. The Nestlé structure from about 2002 is shown in Figure 6.1. The structure shows the typical corporate functions reporting to the CEO. One group of technical functions has been organized under a unit called Nestec. This

Table 6.1: Factors Influencing the Balance of Power in the Matrix Structure

	Strong Geographic Dimension	*Strong Business Dimension*
Amount of cross-border coordination	Low fixed costs (R&D capital, promotions)	High fixed costs
	Heterogeneous markets and unique products	Homogeneous markets and standard products
	Local customers, competitors, suppliers	Global customers, competitors, suppliers
	Low transportability	High transportability
Activity of local institutions	Government active and demanding	Government passive
	Strong unions, local partners	Weak unions, wholly owned subsidiaries
Diversity of international business portfolio	Multiple businesses but single business logic	Multiple businesses and many business logics

unit consists of staff technical functions, such as R&D, operations, and supply chain. These are functional services that are usually charged out to the countries. Another entity reporting to the CEO is the strategic business units. This entity comprises all the product lines that manage the global brands like Nescafe, Nestea, and so on. The business units managing those global brands and product lines are also responsible for new product development projects for products that will be sold in multiple countries. The corporate functions, the technical functions, and the strategic business units are all considered to be lite versions (except finance).

The dominant dimension is the geographic dimension of the structure. Small countries are gathered into regions. Regions and large countries are gathered into zones. In the past ten years, the number of zones has varied from three, as shown, to six. This geographic dimension is the location of the profit

Figure 6.1: Nestlé's Three-Dimensional Matrix

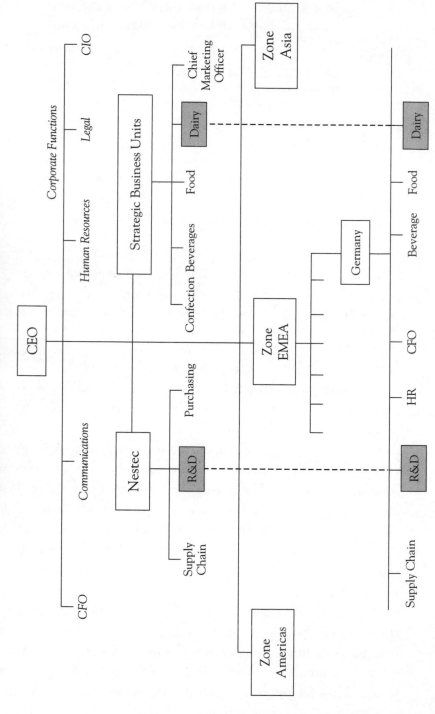

centers. Originally the countries were the building blocks, but recently the regions and zones have increased in strength. The large countries, such as Germany, Japan, and the United States, are still strong profit centers. It is at the level of the large countries that we can see the three-dimensional matrix.

An important point is that a three-dimensional matrix does not mean that people have three bosses. As we will see, the structures are designed so that no one has more than two bosses. The figure shows that in large countries, the entire Nestlé structure is reproduced in microcosm. That is, the German country manager has the same corporate functions, technical functions, and business units reporting to him or her as the CEO. It is the major geographic managers who have to balance the functions and businesses, each of which have two bosses. The CEO is the balancer of the three dimensions.

Nestlé is a good example of a geography-dominant matrix. It has low fixed costs. It spends about 0.5 percent of sales on R&D. Food plants are expensive investments, but large countries and regional clusters of small countries can afford them. Nestlé does spend a lot on advertising global brands. Hence it has strategic business units (SBUs) to coordinate across borders. However, the SBUs are lite entities relative to the countries. Food products are different in each of the heterogeneous markets or countries. For example, there are three different flavors of tomato soup for Switzerland alone. Food products are moderate on the value-to-transport-cost scale. With geography-dominant structures, Nestlé is in a good position to deal with host governments. Finally, Nestlé has a related business portfolio. It is low on the diversity scale. The portfolio is quite manageable by country managers.

This balance can be altered if there are changes in the strategy. For example, Nestlé is emphasizing nutritional products. The priority of nutrition may increase the amount of R&D and new product development activity. If the increase in R&D happens, we will see an increase in the influence of the R&D function and

Figure 6.2: ABB's Geography-Business Matrix (c. 1995)

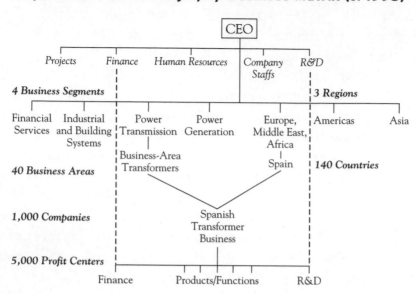

the SBUs. The SBUs will become more active in the new product development process and the R&D budget. In this way, the power of the functions, businesses, and countries can be dialed up and dialed down as needed.

The Balanced Matrix

The balanced matrix is a slight variation on the geography-dominant model. In Figure 6.2, we can see the balanced matrix model patterned after ABB's structure in the 1990s.

The balance between country and business is achieved by having the business unit in a country report to two bosses directly. The functions are placed in the country business unit. They report to the corporate functions and to the country business unit manager. ABB was considered quite successful at running a balanced matrix. One reason was that the balance was achieved by a well-defined division of responsibilities between business and country managers. The company's internal document described these roles and responsibilities:

The scope of responsibility for the business segment and business area managements typically comprise:

Development of a worldwide strategy;

Worldwide results and profitability;

R&D and product development including international coordination and external agreements;

Group internal market allocation schemes and sourcing;

Group internal price strategy and price coordination between countries;

Purchasing coordination;

Product and production allocation;

Transfer of know how in design, production and quality;

Acquisitions, divestments and major investments in agreement with country managers and subject to approval by responsible member of Group management;

Risk Management.

Regional management (country, regional segment, and local unit managers) is responsible for:

Articulating customer based regional strategies—usually within a structured business plan defining specific performance targets—and implementing worldwide segment and business area strategies in the local markets;

Regional results and profitability;

Day-to-day management of individual profit centers;

Human resources development in the regional units;

Building and strengthening relationships with local governments, communities, labor unions and the media;

(Continued)

Ensuring that the customer is not confused by multiple offerings from ABB businesses in his region. This includes clear policies for dealing with composite plant business (joint offerings) and mechanisms for presenting a united ABB front to the customer;

Leveraging ABB's local presence to enhance the Group's global position.

Another reason that the balanced matrix worked at ABB was that the structure fit the strategy. It had a high-fixed-cost business. ABB made power generators, locomotives, and other heavy equipment in capital-intensive factories. It spent between 7 and 8 percent of sales on R&D annually. The products were mostly standard, but with some local modifications. The competitors were becoming global as these industries were consolidating. And the company had a moderately diverse portfolio. All these factors favored a strong business unit structure.

The counterbalance to the business structure was the local customer. Many of ABB's customers were not just local but were state-owned utilities, telecoms, railroads, and oil refineries. ABB estimated that 70 percent of its sales went to government-owned or government-influenced customers. In order to win business, ABB had to be a local business, look like a local business, and have a strong local country manager. The way to run the business was to look and act like a local business but to create and manufacture the products on a global basis. The ABB answer was to organize around a balanced geography-business matrix with strong R&D, operations, and finance functions. Actually, the CEO was the CFO as well. So ABB had achieved a good alignment between strategy and structure.

ABB maintained this balanced matrix organization from 1986 when ABB was created until 1998. During this time, ABB and its CEO received much publicity about executing the matrix when everyone else was having great difficulty with theirs. The CEO cited some other factors in addition to the strategy-structure fit. The first was the accounting system, which could measure the performance of both business and country as well as businesses within a country. ABB had created an accounting system that could measure five thousand profit centers throughout the company. This accounting system allowed ABB to use the planning process for aligning goals between the two sides of the matrix. The other reason was the people. When Asea (A) merged with Brown Boveri (BB) to form ABB, people complained about the complexity of the matrix organization. One of the actions that ABB took was to convene the top four hundred managers once a year and build networks among them. At the meeting in 1988, the CEO asked how many people in the audience were also in the audience at the first meeting in 1986. The estimate was 40 percent. So in two years, 60 percent of the top four hundred were new. Through selection and self-selection, people who could function in a matrix stayed, and those who could not left. So it seems that ABB was successful at a balanced matrix because the company created a complete and aligned Star Model.

In 1998, the CEO left, and a new CEO took over. The new CEO moved ABB away from the balanced matrix to a business-dominant matrix. Of course, the change brought out all the matrix skeptics. They said that they knew all along that a matrix could not work, that ABB had finally gotten smart and organized by business units. My view was quite a different one. I thought that ABB had been smart all along. The matrix had served them well for twelve years. Now the world and ABB's strategy had changed to where a business-dominant matrix would align with both. What had happened? First ABB changed its portfolio. It sold some businesses where the government was the customer (locomotives) and bought some businesses where global companies were the customers (factory automation). Second, the 1990s were a time of deregulation and privatization of ABB's existing customers (utilities and telecoms). So there was less need to be seen as a local supplier and to have strong country managers who could close deals with local governments. There was still a need for a country manager, but there was a greater need for a global business manager. Stronger global businesses and a stronger R&D function were needed to realign the strategy and structure of ABB.

This was also the period of time when European companies adopted the three-dimensional structure, or cube model, shown in Figure 2.3. In addition to Ciba-Geigy and Shell, Philips, Siemens and several other companies all adopted the cube model. These companies were all originally organized around country profit centers. The rise of the European Common Market and then European Union opened up markets, and these companies introduced business units to coordinate across countries. The transition away from countries to a three-dimensional matrix was a difficult one. Through the 1990s, these companies, like ABB, found that global business units and a business-dominant matrix aligned their international strategies and their international structures. Let us now look at the business-dominant international matrix.

The Business-Dominant Matrix

The preceding section described ABB's evolution (as well as that of some other companies) into a business-dominant matrix. The structure of the company would look no different than the one shown in Figure 6.2. What would be different would be the decision-making roles. The business unit managers would be responsible for more decisions, control more of the budget, and have a stronger voice in talent allocation. The business roles would be staffed with the most talented managers. So the various levers of power distribution described in Chapter Five would be used to tilt the matrix toward the business and functional axes.

The reasons for the power shift were many. First, there was increased deregulation and privatization, increasing membership in the WTO, and increasing cross-border trade. Recall that most cross-border trade is intracompany trade. So this increase in trade translated into increases in power and authority for business units and for supply chain functions, and the consequent rise of a global procurement function. Second, there was increased spending on R&D. Asian companies were taking the low-cost end of the business. Western companies focused on new products for the high end of the markets. Again the global business leaders and the R&D function ran the new product development process. Finally, there was the rise of the global customer who wanted to partner with its global suppliers. Once again these cross-border transactions reduced the power and authority of country managers and increased them for global business and global sales account managers.

In summary, companies have followed the trends in globalization when creating international strategies and implementing them through international matrix structures. Initially most companies followed a geography-dominant matrix. Then they transitioned to a balanced matrix and finally to a business-dominant matrix as described. But the business world rarely stands still. Let's look at the evolving international structures since the turn of the century.

Differentiated Structures

Most companies today are moving to differentiated organizational structures. That is, they are organizing differently in different parts of the world and for different businesses. For example, 3M adopted a business-dominant matrix in Europe and the United States and a geography-dominant model in the rest of the world. More companies are adopting similar organization models.

These changes, as usual, are being driven by changes in the world of business. One of the changes is the growth and opportunities in the emerging market countries, especially Brazil,

Russia, India, and China. As companies focus their own growth on these countries, they find that the countries are strange and difficult places to do business. One of the requirements for growth in strange new geographies is a strong local country manager who knows how to do business in the local way. The companies also find that these countries have governments that are active in their economies. State-owned enterprises are the companies' customers, competitors, suppliers, and partners. Again a requirement for success is a strong local country manager to negotiate for the company with these local institutions and to explain the country to the company. Second, there are large question marks surrounding the continued march of globalization. There is increasing protectionism in the United States and Europe. There is the massive transfer of wealth to the Asian and oil-producing countries. The United States and Europe are resisting the investments from these countries' sovereign funds and their state-owned enterprises. Finally, there is the failure of the Doha round of the WTO. Countries are resisting further reductions of tariffs and trade barriers. It appears to be a time for the return of the country manager.

One example is Philips; the Dutch company went from a country-based P&L organization to a balanced matrix to a business unit–based P&L organization over some twenty years. When a new CEO took over early in this decade, he began to reintroduce the countries and the regional dimension to the organization structure. It is still a business-dominated matrix, but the country manager for China reports to the CEO. So it appears that China runs on a balanced matrix model. Like 3M, Philips organizes different parts of the world differently.

Differentiated structures can apply to business as well. Nestlé, as described earlier, runs on a geography-dominant matrix. But Nestlé recently diversified into pet food when it acquired Ralston Purina. More recently it created a separate business unit for nutrition when it acquired Jenny Craig. Both of these new businesses are run with more autonomy than Nestlé's existing businesses. Thus the existing businesses are managed through a geography-dominant matrix, whereas the new businesses are managed through a business-dominant matrix.

In summary, companies are differentiating their matrix structures to allow some countries more autonomy than others. These countries are new, growing markets (to the company) in which the governments are active and state-owned enterprises are common. Strong local country managers are needed to influence the countries and to exercise influence in their companies. Similarly, companies are organizing different businesses differently. They are more willing to manage the complexities of differentiated structures that better align different strategies with different forms of organization.

Other Three-Dimensional Models

Most of the three-dimensional matrix organizations involve the geographic dimension in some way, but some do not. For example, software companies in large countries can achieve scale without expanding internationally. They can organize around functions, product lines, and customer segments. Retailers in large countries also tend to be domestic-only enterprises. Let us look at their implementations of three-dimensional matrix structures.

Wal-Mart, Tesco, and Ikea are exceptions among retailers, as most remain domestic businesses serving local customers. The competitive advantages achieved in one country do not always transfer into new geographies. Wal-Mart and Marks & Spencer both have had difficulties in other countries. Many successful retailers, such as Nordstrom, Best Buy, Target, and Kohl's, remain domestic companies or venture across borders only into Canada.

Retailers have historically seen themselves as a single business that sold a related set of product lines to a customer segment; as such, they all organized on a functional basis, with functions for store operations, marketing, distribution, and merchandising. The merchants or buyers were the dominant function and were organized into product categories—apparel, sporting goods, electronics, home furnishings, lawn and garden, and so on. This category structure was replicated in distribution. Category planners in distribution moved merchandise from the retailers' distribution centers to the stores. Inside the stores, there were departments that also replicated the merchandising category structure. So we could say that the retailers were organized as a function-dominant matrix. This arrangement worked well when retailers were selling their vendors' brands. For example, Sony did the marketing, advertising, product development, and product supply from their factories to the retailers' distribution centers. But everything changed when retailers wanted exclusive assortments and their own brands.

The change proceeded slowly, but eventually retailers created their own functions for design, product development, sourcing, logistics, and marketing. The big change was that the retailers had to develop and coordinate their own supply chains. Typically they created a design center in New York. The apparel designers would build on designs coming out of Europe. The designs then went to product development centers in Hong Kong or Shanghai. In these centers, the detailed specifications would be determined. A sourcing unit would take the detailed designs and select factories in China or elsewhere in Asia for manufacturing. Then a logistics function would manage the supply from the Asian factories to the retailers' distribution centers. So these retailers vertically integrated by adding new functions for design, product development, sourcing, and logistics. Except for logistics, these new functions replicated the product category structure of merchandising. The product categories then formed cross-functional category business teams. These teams formed the function-product matrix that is shown in Figure 6.3. (The figure, which uses Kohl's as an example, shows all the connections for the apparel category.)

Another big change was in the skill set for merchandising category managers. Originally they were buyers. The vendors did

Figure 6.3: Approximation of Kohl's Matrix

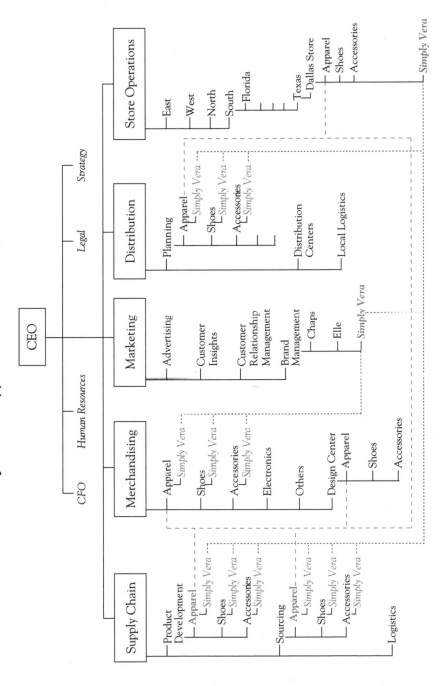

all the supply chain coordination and marketing. With vertical integration, the category managers became full P&L general managers. They needed to manage cross-functional teams with tight time frames on product development and delivery cycles. Some of the existing merchants could make the adjustment, but most could not. Most retailers had to go outside to hire from other retailers or from the vendors. As a result, the product dimension became very much stronger. The structure was still a function-dominant matrix.

The next change has been the licensing of upscale designer brands. Kohl's, for example, has engaged Vera Wang, a fashion designer for very expensive bridal gowns; Ralph Lauren; and *Elle* magazine to create exclusive brands: Simply Vera, Chaps, and Elle. The addition of their brands to the retailers' product lines also requires the addition of brand managers, usually in marketing, to coordinate the brands across product categories and across functions. The team for Vera Wang's Simply Vera brand is shown in Figure 6.3. The brand manager first has to coordinate the look and feel of the brand across product lines. The apparel, shoes, and accessories all have to form an integrated collection. This look and feel needs to be maintained across design, product development, and manufacturing. Then in the stores themselves, the shopping experience needs to complete the brand's look and feel. When volume permits, there may be a Simply Vera store within a store. Collectively these categories and functions all work together to achieve the profitability of the brand. These brands and brand teams form the third dimension of the matrix. The priority is still functions first, categories second, and brands third. Thus retailers are a good example of a brand, product, and function three-dimensional matrix organization.

Summary

This chapter has described the three-dimensional matrix. Most matrix structures in three dimensions arise from doing business internationally. We saw that the international structures are of three types: geography dominant, balanced, and business dominant. The strength of functions varies with the percentage of sales invested in R&D, the amount of cross-border trade (supply chain), and the investments in advertising for global brands (marketing). We also discussed the strategic factors that favored business-dominant or geography-dominant structures (high fixed costs and active host governments, respectively). The chapter concluded with discussion of differentiated structures whereby different matrix models are used in different parts of the world, and of three-dimensional matrix models employed by retailers.

As we will see in Chapter Seven, companies have not stopped at the three-dimensional matrix. Four and more dimensions have been added. In these circumstances it is the customer that is forcing more complexity on companies.

7

MORE COMPLEX MATRIX STRUCTURES

In this chapter, we examine the more complex matrix designs. These designs involve four or more dimensions of organization structure at the top of the company. First we look at the addition of global accounts to the three-dimensional matrix models that we explored in Chapter Six. Whether companies had mastered the three-dimensional design or not, their customers often pushed them into adding a fourth dimension, a customer dimension. The second part of the chapter focuses on the front-back hybrid organizational form. Many companies that added global or national accounts grew them into multifunctional customer-facing units. The back ends were organized around global product lines. There is usually a matrix organization that ties the front and back units together.

Global Account Teams

Just when I think that I have seen the limit of organizational complexity, I am engaged to work with a more complex structure. In the Preface, I mentioned a project that I started when I was on the faculty at IMD in 1998. During that project, I interviewed ABB's leadership when they were adding a customer dimension in the form of global accounts. Some customers, such as DaimlerChrysler and Shell, wanted a single account manager through which they could coordinate their global purchases. ABB started with a few global accounts, which had grown to over sixty when I last talked with ABB management.

Figure 7.1: ABB's Geography-Business Matrix with Global Accounts (c. 1995)

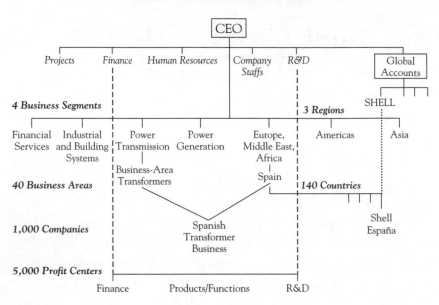

The structure that ABB added is shown in Figure 7.1. At the corporate level, it added a global accounts unit. Then customers that wanted a single point of contact had a global account manager who reported to the head of global accounts and to the country manager in which the customer had its headquarters. In every country where purchasing took place, an account manager was created to coordinate the customer's purchases across all the ABB businesses in the country. Typically the local global account manager reported to the country manager in order to coordinate across all the business units in the country. Again we see that four dimensions do not lead to four bosses. Each matrix structure involves only two bosses.

The Front-Back Hybrid Model

Very often the creation of global or national account units is the first step toward a customer-focused business unit. This was the case at ABB, P&G, and Citibank. They have created a structure that is now known as the front-back model. The customer-focused structures designed by ABB, P&G, and Citibank create two, somewhat parallel line organizations: one focused on the customer (the front end) and a second focused on products (the back end). Several other types of companies are also adopting this kind of organization; the objective in all cases is to achieve a customer focus and responsiveness concurrent with global-scale economies. When the front end is based on countries, the objective is to achieve the elusive global and local combination. The simultaneous achievement of these conflicting objectives results from solving the management challenge of effectively linking the customer front end with the product back end. Matrix organization structures are instrumental in this effective linkage.

The front-back model is a type of dual structure in which both halves are multifunctional units. The structure for a manufacturer of diesel engines for ships is shown in Figure 7.2. The front half (on the right side), which is organized around the customer, can be a geographic or country structure, or it can be focused on some market segmentation scheme, such as industries. The back half (on the left), which is usually organized around products or product lines, supplies all the customer units and achieves global scale.

In the company's language, the countries are called market companies, and the product lines are called product companies. Both the product and the market companies shown in Figure 7.2 are multifunctional profit centers, although each type of company (whether it's a country or a product line) has different functions. The front-back model separates the value chain for the business. The functions closest to the customer—the front-end functions like sales, local marketing, customer service, and technical support—are focused and organized around the customer's needs. Those functions upstream from the customer—R&D, operations, and product marketing—are organized to achieve product excellence and scale. In the example, none of these business functions are shared or have two bosses,

Figure 7.2: Front–Back Hybrid Structure

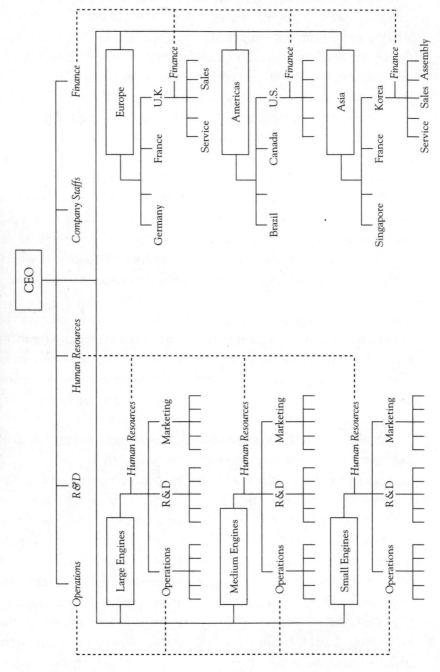

so it is not a matrix organization like the former ABB structure. Neither is it a country organization. The large-engine product company, although located in the United Kingdom, is a separate profit center from the U.K. market company. Product companies are structured to serve all market companies equally. Serving all market companies distinguishes the front-back from the global business unit structure. Figure 7.3 contrasts the product flow of the front-back model with that of the business units of General Electric. GE's profit centers have dedicated sales and service functions for each business unit; the diesel engine supplier uses its sales and service functions to sell and service all its products in its market companies. The front-back model requires a much more complicated product flow than the business unit model does. The front-back is therefore a hybrid; it is not a country-based structure, nor is it a global business structure, but rather a combination of the two.

The corporate functions form a matrix across the product company and market company profit centers. The operations and R&D functions form a matrix across the product companies. The HR and finance functions form a matrix across both product and market companies. So the diesel engine company has a three-dimensional structure: product, geographies, and functions. But only the functions form a matrix across both product and market companies.

Some form of matrix is usually employed to tie the front and the back together; the diesel engine supplier illustrates the concept. The corporate function–profit center matrix just described is one form. In the 1980s, diesel engines began to be used to supply electric power, and some towns and factories found that they could use a smaller power plant than those supplied by power-generation companies like ABB. (The company whose organization is shown in Figure 7.2 focused on this smaller power market.) A diesel engine supplier could get an engine running and delivering power more quickly and cheaply than a power-generation company could. The diesel engine company

Figure 7.3: Front-Back Model Compared with Business Unit Model

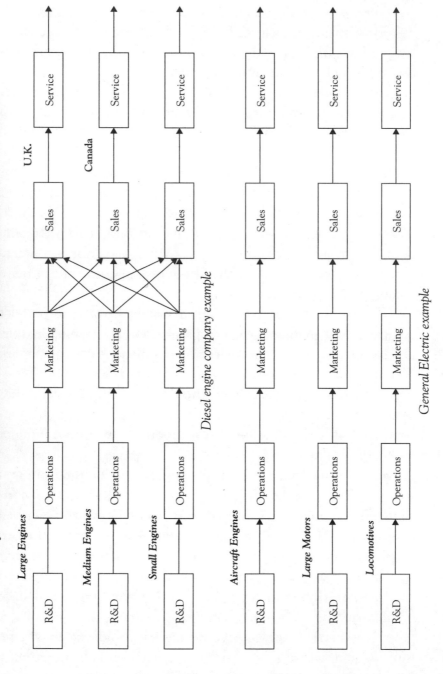

Large Engines

Medium Engines

Small Engines

U.K.

Canada

Diesel engine company example

Aircraft Engines

Large Motors

Locomotives

General Electric example

R&D — Operations — Marketing — Sales — Service

had to make product modifications so that its engines could more efficiently generate electricity. Fully half the current diesel engine sales are to the power market (the remainder are for ship propulsion). Because the purchasers of power engines want only an electrical source and not all the headaches of running a power plant, the engine supplier started a service business to operate power plants for cities and factories, as well as to provide engine maintenance. The resulting organization is shown in Figure 7.4.

The diesel engine supplier has added two new businesses—power and service—to what was the lone marine engine business. These global businesses link the product companies and the market companies, through shared activities that form a matrix organization. For example, sales in the market companies is now specialized and divided into the marine market, the power market, and the service market. The marine sales unit in a country is shared and reports to the global marine business manager and the country manager. In the product companies, product development, some manufacturing and assembly, and product marketing are now organized by power, service, and marine; within the product companies, there is sufficient volume to allow a business specialization. Purchasing and some component manufacturing remain separate and serve all businesses. The R&D and manufacturing resources are shared resources, collected into the product companies. The business manager within the product company reports to the global business manager and to the head of the product company. The businesses form a matrix structure across the product and market companies, with the business resources shared. The addition of the business matrix makes the diesel engine company a four-dimensional structure of functions, geographies (markets), products, and businesses.

In some industries, the front-back hybrid form has been around for some time, although it was not referred to as front-back. The investment banking business has always had relationship management and product management components, but the front-back model now occurs in all types of businesses. What is causing this organizational form to be the structure of choice?

Figure 7.4: Combination of Front-Back and Matrix Models

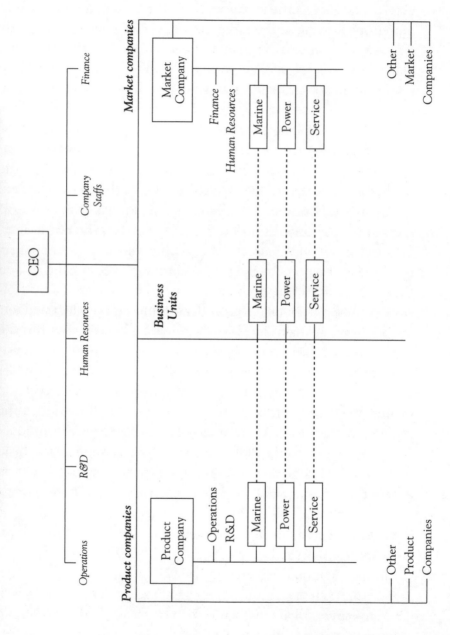

A number of forces are pushing companies into the front-back structure, but the dominant one is the customer (see Galbraith, 2005). A major effect of global competition has been a shift of power in the buyer-seller relationship to the buyer, who has learned how to use this power and now demands more value and more attentive service than previously. Sellers are responding to these demands by organizing their activities around customers and customer segments, although in many industries it is impossible to align and dedicate all functional activities to a customer segment and form a self-contained business unit; the semiconductor industry is an example.

Semiconductor manufacturers must now customize their products for buyers in the telecommunications, defense, computer, and automotive industries; these manufacturers have created sales, service, application engineering, and product design units dedicated to customers in these industries. However, a semiconductor factory now costs $3 billion or more, and it is impossible to build a factory for each customer segment. Therefore product units, which supply all customer segments, are created for the factories, as well as for product engineering and supporting activities. These product units achieve global scale, while the customer units achieve focus, customization, and responsiveness. As mentioned earlier, this is the primary objective of the structure: to simultaneously achieve customer focus and responsiveness as well as product excellence and scale. The front-back is a structure designed for mass customization. It is mass in the back and customized in the front. The local customer, with uniquely local needs, can be supplied on a global scale. This structure permits the supplier to be simultaneously global and local.

The following are factors that cause a multiproduct company to choose the front-back structure:

- Customers can buy all products.
- Customers want a single point of contact.

- Customers want a sourcing partnership.
- Customers want solutions and systems, not components and stand-alone products.
- Opportunities exist for cross-selling and bundling.
- Value-added is becoming increasingly customer specific.
- Advantage can be gained through superior knowledge about customers and customer segments.

Let us look more closely at these factors.

The pressure for a market focus (and a separate structure) starts when customers buy—or can buy—all products. (If products are all purchased by different customers in different countries, there is no pressure for separate customer structures.) When customers can buy all products, the question arises of whether each product group needs its own sales force—all of whom call on the same customer. Would it not be more economical to have one sales force sell all products to the customer? The answer depends, in part, on how the customer wants to do business. Some customers have different buyers purchasing different products from the same vendor; these companies may prefer to have separate, product-knowledgeable salespeople calling on separate, product-knowledgeable buyers. Some products may be sold to the customer end user and not to buyers from purchasing at all. Increasingly, however, customers are pooling their purchases and negotiating a total, single contract with multiproduct vendors. These customers want a single point of contact in the vendor organization for communication, negotiation, and coordination to lower their joint costs. These single interfaces are the beginning of the front-end customer structure.

An increasing number of customers are adopting sourcing policies like those of the auto industry—that is, they prefer to have fewer, closer, and longer-term vendor relationships; they choose one or two vendors for a product and dedicate their entire volume to those vendors, who become their partners.

In return, the customer may prefer—and some will insist—that the vendor create a strong local manager or a dedicated organizational unit with whom it can conduct its business; this unit becomes a front-end customer unit.

Some customers want to buy systems rather than products. Wells Fargo Bank is buying products when it orders twenty-five servers from IBM, but Wells Fargo may actually want to buy a consumer banking system. A system consists of many products—desktop computers, teller terminals, automated teller machines, high-volume transaction processors, servers, disk-drive storage—that are all manufactured by different units at IBM or its partners. When buying a system, Wells Fargo does not want a collection of products but a banking system that works. As a result, IBM will do the systems integration for customers like Wells Fargo who do not want to do it themselves. Thus vendors like IBM need a systems integration capability, which may also become a front-end customer function or part of a global services business unit.

Customers who do not currently buy all of a vendor's products may provide cross-selling opportunities for the vendor; by packaging ("bundling") products together for a single price, the vendor may win an increased share of the customer's business. Software companies create "suites" of programs in this way for selected segments. Citibank relationship managers package foreign exchange and cash management for global customers. Cross-selling and bundling usually require a single customer-focused unit in the front end to create and price the package for the customer.

The examples just described illustrate that more value-adding activities are being created that are best located in the front-end structure and focused on the local customer or global customer segment. In the past, sales was the one activity organized around the customer, but more customer-specific services and software are now being added. PPG used to sell paint to automobile manufacturers; today, it sells paint, provides application software for choosing paints, and runs the entire painting operation for General Motors. As the economies of developed countries become service and information oriented, companies will continue to add service and software as a source of growth. These services, which typically require customization for market segments and customers, are being located in the front-end local, or customer, structure.

Many companies are recognizing that a local customer or customer segment structure allows them to create superior information and knowledge about customers and to form close relationships with them. If the knowledge and relationships can be converted to superior solutions, products, and services, the segment focus will become a competitive advantage.

The use of the front-back hybrid has spread to many industries. The investment and commercial banks have customer-facing units organized around customer segments (industries) and countries. The back end is organized around global product lines (equities, fixed-income loans, bonds, treasury products, cash management, and so on). The usual corporate functions and operations complete the four-dimensional model. Consumer goods companies like P&G and Unilever have implemented the front-back model. Their customer-facing units are largely geographic regions but include a unit for global customers, such as Wal-Mart, Carrefour, Tesco, and Metro. The back ends are the global product lines. The products are matrixed into the regions and customer units. Then the functions form a matrix across the global businesses, the regions, and the customer units, as shown in Figure 1.2. This front-back structure is rapidly replacing the balanced matrix structure as companies add the fourth dimension that focuses on customers.

Summary

This chapter focused on the four-dimensional matrix and its hybrid form, the front-back. The fourth or customer dimension is added at the insistence of the customers themselves. In the case of Citibank, large global customers like Nestlé simply did not want to deal with one hundred Citibanks in one hundred countries. Sometimes the customer dimension is a lite version, like the global accounts shown in Figure 7.1. But more often companies are going to multifunctional customer-facing units and global product back ends. A good example is IBM. In the next chapter, I analyze the example of IBM in detail. Besides being a good example of the front-back, IBM has added two additional dimensions of complexity.

8

THE IBM STRUCTURE

This chapter analyzes the structure of IBM in some detail. I conducted interviews with the managers of IBM several times during my tenure at IMD. I analyze the company here because it is probably the most complex organization that I have seen. It also has examples of two- and three-dimensional matrix models embedded in it. IBM provides us with a good review of the structures that we saw in the earlier chapters.

The IBM Front-Back Hybrid

The most complex organization that I have encountered is IBM's. The structure that I will describe had six dimensions to it (as of around 2002). As shown in Figure 8.1, IBM is organized around functions, products, solutions, customers, geographies, and channels. It also is organized around a customer-facing front end and a product and solution back end. The front end of the structure consists of regions, customer segments based on industries, and channel partners through which IBM sells to its customers. The back end consists of the product lines, which are grouped under hardware, software, and services. Generic or cross-industry solutions are organized as part of global services. For example, customer relationship management (CRM) systems are solutions consisting of a combination of hardware, software, and services and are sold to customers in all industries. Solutions that are industry specific are organized as part of the industry groups. This structure allows IBM to achieve global scale and leverage in the back end and local adaptation and customization in the front end. Indeed, the front-back structure is a means for implementing mass customization strategies.

Figure 8.1: IBM's Front-Back Structure

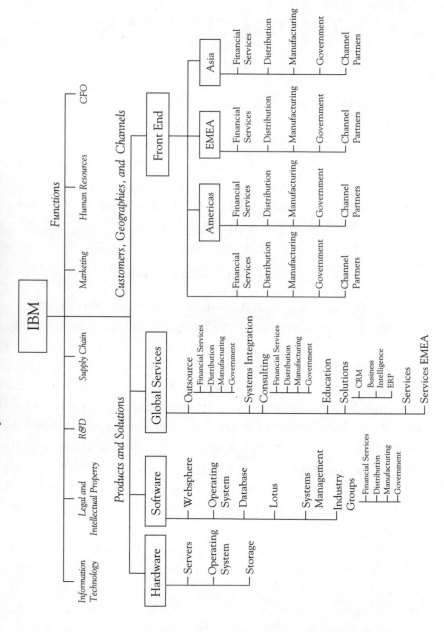

We can see from Figure 8.1 how IBM uses the matrix organization to provide linkages across the dimensions of the structure. First, the front end is a matrix of customer segments across regions. Four of the twelve customer segments (financial services, distribution, manufacturing, and government) are shown here. The customer segments are a direct channel served by IBM's own sales force. The fifth unit shown, channel partners, comprises the indirect channels served by the sales forces from the partners. The customer segment heads lead the strategy and customer planning activities. The people are located in the regions. So the regional heads lead the tactical activities of allocating talent across the regional customer projects. The second linkage is between the front and back. When there is sufficient volume in a segment, the product lines can create segment-specific units and dedicate people to them. In software, outsourcing, and consulting there are units dedicated to the segments. These units report primarily to the product lines, but secondarily are part of the company-wide industry segments. A great deal of coordination takes place horizontally between the front and back customer segments.

The front end of the structure is a matrix design consisting primarily of regions and industry groups formed around the top thousand global customers. Figure 8.2 shows the structure from the perspective of one of the industry groups—financial services. The financial services industry group is further subdivided into insurance, capital markets (investment banks), and banking. Also reporting to the industry head are the regional financial services leaders. They also report to their respective regional heads. Some very large accounts, such as Citigroup, report to the head of the industry group. In addition to being large, Citigroup has businesses in banking, insurance, and investment banking. Finally, the usual functions like finance and HR report to the global industry head as well as to their corporate functional leaders. Another key functional unit is the industry marketing group.

Figure 8.2: Global Financial Services Structure

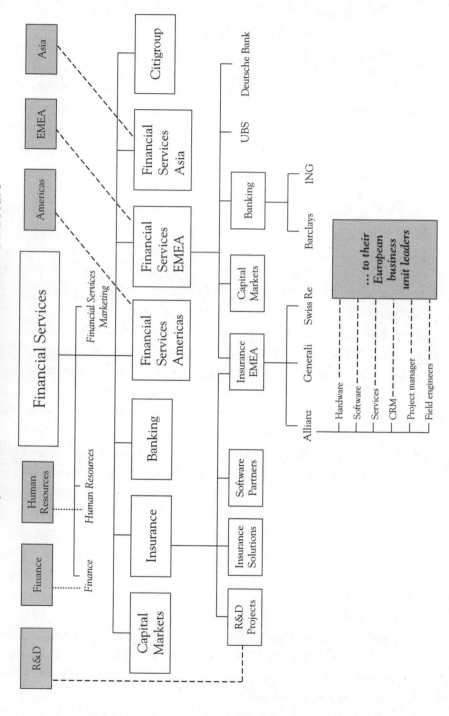

The customer accounts are mostly organized under the regional financial services heads. The insurance accounts report to the insurance regional leader, who in turn reports to both the regional financial services head and the global head of insurance. The large accounts like Allianz of Germany are serviced with an account team. When there is a sufficient volume of business, full-time salespeople for hardware, software, and services are assigned to the account. When a customer is considering a solution like a CRM system, a solutions salesperson is assigned to the account as well. Rounding out the account team is a project manager who gathers an extended team when a proposal is being prepared or a solution is being installed. Field application engineers are also dedicated to accounts in proportion to the volume of activity. All salespeople work for the account manager and also for the regional sales managers for hardware, software, and services.

The front-end industry groups are not just sales and marketing functions. The global insurance unit shown in Figure 8.2 manages R&D projects, develops insurance-specific solutions, and recruits independent software vendors who create software products for the insurance industry. IBM currently spends about 30 percent of its R&D budget on joint projects with customers. It has an insurance research center as part of the industry groups and part of the IBM research labs, a two-dimensional matrix within a matrix. The labs are developing an insurance application architecture along with forty insurance companies. The global insurance unit also has an engagement lab in Belgium called the Insurance Solution Development Center. At this center, they develop solutions by working with lead customers and software partners. An example is the collaborative Internet sales and marketing solution.

So the front-end industry groups are really industry-focused business units. They create strategies and develop solutions and applications that are customized for their industry customers. In so doing, they call upon all the resources from the product lines and functions of the corporation and from global and local partners. At the time of my interviews, the global insurance business was over $5 billion and growing.

Looking at the financial services segment shown in Figure 8.2, we can see how IBM further uses the matrix organization to provide links between the many dimensions of the structure. The first link is to the usual corporate functions (for example, HR and finance), which are matrixed across all the line units. Second, the figure shows how the segments are further subdivided into subsegments and then global customer accounts, which are linked in a matrix across the regions. In a third link, the customer accounts are organized around sales teams consisting of sales representatives from the product lines and solutions units. These salespeople report to the customer account managers and to the sales managers in the product lines and solutions. Finally, there are functional activities that are dedicated to the segment, such as the financial services marketing and insurance R&D units. These units report into their respective corporate functions as well as to the financial services segment. Thus each segment has its links to the product lines, solutions, regions, functions, and channels (although these were not shown).

The regional unit is the other part of the front-end matrix. The EMEA region is shown in Figure 8.3. The industry groups formulate global strategies; the regions are responsible for tactical execution. The regions are IBM in microcosm. Reporting to the regional manager are product lines (mostly salespeople in hardware and software), industry groups, country heads, and functions. All the product lines, functions, and industry groups report to the region head and to their respective global leaders. A main task of the region is the allocation of talent. There is always a talent category that is in short supply. There was a shortage of SAP programmers, then a dearth of experts in secure transactions over the Internet. The regional management team allocates talent according to priorities set by the industry groups. The country managers are relationship managers or ambassadors in their country. They

Figure 8.3: IBM Europe, Middle East, and Africa (EMEA) Front-End Structure

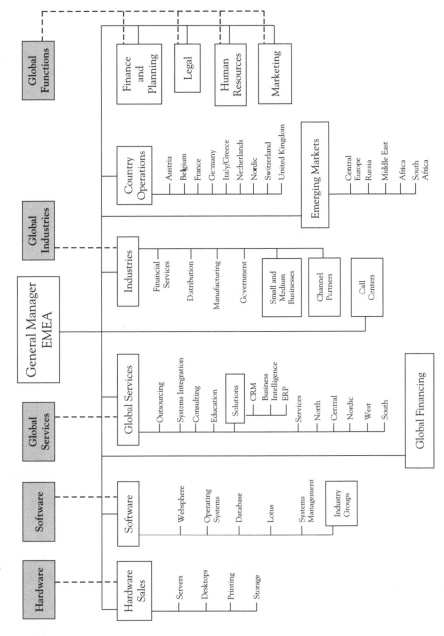

represent IBM to the local institutions and communities. They also surface opportunities for the industry groups. The country managers are stronger in countries where the government is active in the economic process, as in Russia and Egypt. So the region is a tactical integrator of a four-dimensional matrix of products, industries, countries, and functions.

In summary, IBM was a six-dimensional organization at the time of my interviews. It had adopted a front-back structure with extensive matrix relationships linking the front and back units. In this structure, the back end is the full P&L. In the front end, the segments and regions have gross profit measures because the cost of goods sold is unique to the back. Since the interviews, IBM has added two corporation-wide initiatives: business on demand and pervasive computing (wireless). It continues to push the limits of complexity.

More Complexity?

When you read that IBM has added two more dimensions, you have to scratch your head and ask, "Is there no limit?" In IBM's case, there does not seem to be a limit. Why not? There are probably several reasons.

First, in many cases the benefits outweigh the costs. In the case of pervasive computing, there is a single but talented individual doing the work. He has a contact in each of the major units. Collectively these contacts form the pervasive computing team. For this work, IBM gets some insight as to what is going on across the company. The network spreads the word across all of IBM. Some people are energized by new things like pervasive computing and volunteer. At any point IBM can review the work and terminate it if there is little to show for it. If there is potential, the company can add more people and investment and scale it up to a serious dimension to be added to the IBM matrix. On the customer dimension, even a mediocre implementation may be seen as valuable by those customers who want a single point of contact. It saves them from having to deal with thirty-seven sales forces. So in many cases the value may be worth the time and cost of the effort.

A second reason may be that customers use relative criteria when valuing the efforts of different suppliers. Even if the IBM service seems to be mediocre on an absolute scale, the customer compares it to services from HP and Fujitsu-Siemens. IBM may be superior. In order for HP to create the service, it would have to organize into a four-dimensional structure just like that used by IBM. Until then, IBM only has to execute better than HP in order to win the business.

The third reason is that companies keep inventing new information and decision processes that enable the management of more complex structures. These information and decision processes are the subject matter of Part Three.

Summary

This chapter examined the IBM structure in some detail. The company uses a front-back model to implement six dimensions of the business, and uses matrix designs throughout its structure to make key linkages. IBM serves as an example of how these complex strategies can be implemented.

Part Three

COMPLETING THE STAR MODEL

In Part Three, we address the processes, rewards, and people portions of the Star Model. Indeed, one of the reasons for an increased success rate in implementing matrix organizations is that companies have learned to create a complete and aligned Star Model for the matrix. In this part of the book, we examine the best practices used by companies that are successful at matrix organization.

The complex structures described in Chapter Eight always leave people wondering not just how these organizations work but how they can work at all. How do they get anything done? How can IBM, for example, deliver solutions to customers with a six- or eight-dimensional matrix organization? The answer is that these companies employ management processes that align the goals and priorities of the various dimensions of the matrix. These processes vary from using informal personal networks to holding elaborate large-scale meetings of eight hundred people or more. Increasingly it is the planning and resource allocation processes that are central to the setting of priorities and the matching of talent and funds with the best opportunities. But the successful implementers of matrix designs make extensive use of both horizontal and vertical processes to coordinate all the dimensions of the structure.

The communication processes across the different sides of the matrix are the subject of Chapter Nine. Decisions related to setting joint goals and performing joint evaluations force the conversations that matter across the matrix. The key conversations are those between the two bosses of the person who has the dual reporting relationship.

The planning processes are the subject of Chapters Ten and Eleven. These processes run off of spreadsheets that display the links between the different sides of the matrix. The cells in the spreadsheet indicate where shared goals need to be articulated. These processes align the goals of the different dimensions of the matrix and focus them on working together. This alignment is key to establishing collaboration. The different sides of the matrix can then focus on how to meet the goals. If there is no alignment, the different sides cannot work together; they argue continually about unaligned goals or pursue their own goals and interests. As companies have added more dimensions to the matrix, the number of people involved in achieving alignment has escalated. The large-scale meeting is now being employed to resolve the conflicts and align the goals of the multidimensional matrix designs.

The planning process to achieve alignment becomes just an exercise if it is not backed up by the HR policies and practices of the firm. Some of the best examples of HR practices that support matrix organizations occur in professional services firms. They recruit and select people who will fit their type of matrix. The partners devote time and energy to developing and promoting talent. All associates, as well as partners, receive full and fair assessments of their individual performance. A full assessment comprises subjective assessments of hard-to-measure performance behaviors like collaboration, as well as more objective assessments of whether the individual is meeting quantitative shared goals determined during the planning process. These best practices are described in Chapter Twelve.

In Chapter Thirteen, we address the topic of leadership in a matrix organization. Although leadership is always important, there are some specific challenges to leading in a matrix. If the company portfolio consists of a set of autonomous businesses or countries, there is little need for a top management team. The CEO can interact with the business leaders on a one-on-one basis. In a matrix of any type, the leaders are interdependent. There is a need for a leadership team and collaboration among team members. This collaboration is critical to the resolution of conflicts. The matrix structure naturally generates differences of opinion, and the more dimensions there are in the matrix, the more differences of opinion there will be. The leader of a matrix needs to manage these differences into an aligned set of shared goals. The purpose of the planning process is to provide leaders with the platform they need in order to resolve the natural conflicts that arise with the matrix structure. Another role of the leader is that of the balancer of power. The distribution of power internally needs to be aligned with the external threats and opportunities. As the external realities change, the power distribution needs to change with them. The balancing of power is a continuous leadership role requirement.

Another leadership requirement is to manage the change process when implementing new matrix designs. Chapter Fourteen is devoted to the change process. Because matrix is an inherently collaborative form of organization, the change process should be a collaborative effort as well. During the transition, the management should learn the skills it will need to run the matrix. The chapter includes a detailed example of a complete change process.

9

COMMUNICATION IN THE MATRIX

Successful implementation of the matrix form of organization is very dependent on effective communication across the various dimensions of the structure. The reason is that the addition of new dimensions to the structure increases interdependence between structural units. The communication is needed to facilitate coordination of that interdependence. For example, the implementation of national accounts increases the interdependence across sales regions. When there are no national accounts, sales regions can act independently. They can set delivery dates and prices guided only by company policy. But if a region makes generous delivery promises or price discounts to a national account, that customer will want the same delivery policy and price discounts in all regions. The other regions may disagree. So decisions in one region now impact all regions in which the national account customer is present. The company now needs communication and coordination across regions.

Much of the communication on which a matrix depends is informal communication leading to voluntary coordination. This informal communication is based on personal networks and trusting relationships between people on the different sides of the matrix. These networks and relationships will not form in a company characterized by silos. The leaders' task is to knock down silos wherever they create barriers to effective communication. Many of the ways to eliminate barriers are practices controlled by HR. I discuss these practices in the "Social Capital" section in Chapter Twelve. In this chapter, I introduce some techniques to foster informal communication and network building.

Some additional communication links are matrix-specific links that are often of a more formal nature. Communication between the two bosses on different sides of the matrix is essential. Many companies do not leave these contacts to chance and build them in. The team processes as well are often formalized and channeled into the preparation of plans leading to joint goals. Let us examine these informal and formal communication practices.

Informal Communication

As mentioned earlier, matrix organizations contain very interdependent structures. They require intense communication at all the interfaces. Not all of this communication can be planned. It must arise voluntarily and be conducted naturally and informally. And it will arise naturally when there are personal networks and trusting relationships across the different dimensions of the matrix. These networks need to be valued and promoted by management.

A good example of these informal networks in use is BMW. It is organized in a manner similar to Chrysler, as shown in Figure 2.4. Like the other auto companies, BMW cannot afford to have barriers to communication across its functions. It is very dependent on effective cross-functional coordination in launching a constant stream of new products in short time frames. As many companies do, BMW builds networks through the gatherings of the top 150 managers and through cross-functional leadership development programs.

BMW is also known for its cross-functional career development path. Large numbers of its potential leaders take cross-functional assignments. These moves occur at all levels. In summer 2007, for example, the CFO became the global sales director. However, it is the "knight's move" pattern of career development that is discussed the most. Career paths in BMW tend to mimic the movement pattern of a knight on a chessboard. That is, leaders first move up in their function and then over to a new function. Then they move up in that function before moving over to another function. In this way, leaders get broad experience, learn the languages of different functions, and develop multifunctional personal relationships. They then use this network to engage in informal communications when needed throughout their careers.

The other feature of BMW is the use of colocation of functional teams that are working on a new product design project. Most auto companies colocate now, but BMW has a long history of locating cross-functional project teams in a "prototype factory." That is, when launching a new 3 Series platform, for example, all functions doing design work on the 3 Series locate their design teams in the factory—the engineers designing the car, the manufacturing process design team, and the team designing the marketing program, as well as teams designing the sales program, the dealer training program, and the employee training program. It is during the design process that communication and coordination are most intense. These teams stay together from the start through to the launch of the new product. Then the 5 Series team moves into the prototype factory.

Thus through all these practices, the leadership at BMW builds networks, destroys silos, and fosters informal communication and coordination.

Formal Communication

In addition to creating a foundation of personal networks and informal communication, the effective implementers of matrix organizations selectively add formal communication links. These links can be illustrated using the sales organization example that we have used in other chapters.

The formal communication links are shown in the example of a matrix of national (or global) accounts and sales regions.

An example structure was shown in Figure 1.3. A simplified version is repeated in Figure 9.1 to accentuate the relations between the two sides of the matrix. It is a simple matrix with the national accounts manager and the regional sales manager reporting to the national sales manager. The regional national account manager manages the relationship and sales to the national account in the region. The account has sufficient volume to justify four salespeople in the region that is shown.

The two-headed arrow A in the figure highlights the communication relationship between the national account manager and the regional sales manager. Effective dialogue between these two managers prevents conflicts from arising in the first place. And if conflicts do arise, dialogue prevents them from

Figure 9.1: Communication Required Between the Two Sides of a Simple Matrix

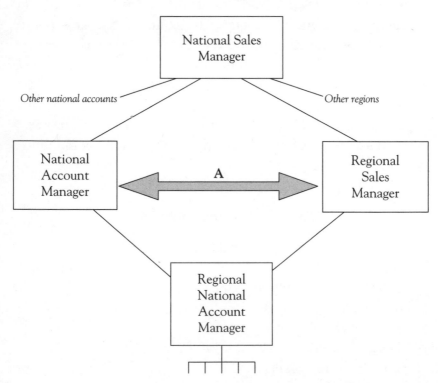

growing and from being dropped on the two-boss manager, the regional national account manager. This dialogue is probably the most important communication link in the matrix structure. Certainly it is the most damaging one if it is absent. The link is also enhanced when the two-boss manager is also brought in to make it a three-way conversation.

The absence of this link between peers is usually revealing. It may signify a power struggle, a passive resistance to change, or both. If the national accounts are being added to the structure, the regional sales managers may resent the intrusion into their territory. A common ploy for regional managers is to avoid talking with the new national account managers. The new national account people are then deprived of important news from the field. The lack of timely information reduces their effectiveness. Then the regional managers can say, "We have tried these national account managers, and they have only increased our cost of sales with no improvements." The "keep them dumb" tactic is quite effective at reducing the effectiveness of any new matrix dimension. The new managers often do not know that they are being set up to fail.

The dialogue between the peers on different sides of the matrix is an important indicator of the health of a matrix. When there is none, that is the time for leadership to intervene to create conversations. The usual practice is to require joint selection and joint evaluations of the two-boss manager by the managers on both sides of the matrix. I'll discuss the details of how this works in the following sections.

Joint Decisions

One way to encourage dialogue between peers is to ask them to make joint decisions. A best practice in matrix organizations is to have the peers select the two-boss manager. In Figure 9.1, the regional and national accounts managers would jointly select the regional national account manager. The joint selection process forces the peers to identify the skills needed, discuss what the person is to do, and compare available candidates. It is important for them to agree on such issues as what the person is expected to do—prior to his or her beginning the work. The joint selection discussion gets the peers to share a concept of what the role expectations are. In short, it allows them to go on maneuvers before using live ammunition.

Another joint decision is to set the goals for the two-boss manager. These will be the goals against which the manager will be held accountable. Like the selection decision, the goals decision requires that the peers engage in a dialogue between themselves and with the two-boss manager prior to when activity begins. The dialogue allows the peers to sort out possible conflicts before they become a reality.

The purpose of the joint goals is to have those goals, rather than either of the bosses, manage the two-boss manager. Useless discussions of dotted and solid lines are thus converted into conversations about what outcomes and goals are desired. The arrow B in Figure 9.2 illustrates the idea that the goals will drive the behavior of the regional national account manager, not commands from either of the two bosses.

The joint decisions, like the responsibility chart, engage the different sides of the matrix in dialogues prior to implementation. These activities are preparatory and allow for the two sides to sort out expectations, identify risks, share their concerns, and think through contingency plans. These are exactly the kinds of discussions that are needed to build relationships and develop a level of trust between the two sides of the matrix. The relationship is then the basis for ongoing dialogues once the matrix is launched and activity begins.

Joint Evaluations

Once the joint selection and joint goal setting have been accomplished, the next step is the joint evaluation of the two-boss

Figure 9.2: Goals Drive the Behavior of the Two-Boss Manager

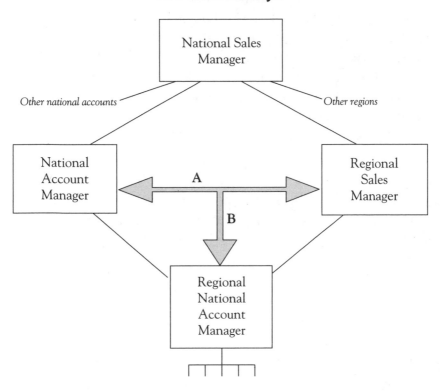

manager by both sides of the matrix. Following the company's performance management system, it is best if the two managers together engage in a face-to-face discussion with the two-boss manager. Some goals will be more important to one or the other of the managers, but the prior joint decisions should have laid the foundation for the joint performance assessment.

Another best practice is to have the national sales manager and the top team assess all the people at the level of the two-boss manager. This team assessment was used successfully at most units in Digital Equipment's matrix organization. This approach takes more work, but more people participate in the process of making subjective judgments. The team can also apply a more consistent standard across the entire unit. There is usually some work needed to get the group to behave as a team and to make tough, candid performance assessments in an open setting. The process can easily be subverted by an implicit or explicit norm of "When you talk about your people, I'll be quiet. When I talk about my direct reports, you be quiet."

During these discussions, some rules of engagement are usually needed. A manager cannot make a blanket statement like "He's a loser." Managers need to cite specific behaviors and evidence to back up their assessments. The process can be facilitated by HR personnel. One of the HR function's jobs is to manage this process and see that it works effectively. If tough issues are to be confronted, the necessary pre-meeting discussions can be conducted. The process also requires that the members of the top team know everyone and look at performance from the point of view of the whole unit. But this process, when properly conducted, will arrive at complete assessments of people's behavior in a matrix organization. People who are self-promoters are more likely to be unmasked, as will dysfunctional behaviors. The discussion is also a team dialogue about performance of the whole unit and the subunits that add up to the total. As companies move to performance management systems, which consider not just what a person accomplishes but how he or she did it, these types of processes are very valuable. We look at more detailed descriptions of matrix-friendly performance management systems in Chapter Eleven.

Summary

Making a matrix work is not about structure. It is not about who has the solid line and who has the dotted line. It is about management communication and relationships between the two sides of the matrix (recall that even six-dimensional structures result in two-boss, two-sided matrix situations). It is about having conversations that matter. To guarantee that these conversations take place, the use of responsibility charts (discussed in

Chapter Five) and management processes for joint selection, goal setting, and evaluation are essential. The employment of these joint activities would appear to be common sense. I take the time to write about them because they are not common practice.

These formal contacts between the two sides of the matrix supplement multiple informal contacts. The practices used at BMW are good examples of breaking down silos, building relationships, and fostering voluntary communications in informal networks. All communication is based on a foundation of personal relationships and trust. Some additional practices for building relationships and trust are presented in Chapter Twelve.

10

PLANNING AND COORDINATION PROCESSES

The successful execution of matrix organizations, especially those with multiple dimensions, is dependent on robust planning and resource allocation processes. These processes accomplish three objectives. The first objective is to align the goals of the different dimensions to work together. The more dimensions that are present, the greater the likelihood of fragmentation and of every dimension going in its own direction. The second objective is to resolve the conflicts that will arise as a consequence of each dimension's having its own ideas and preferences. The third objective is to prioritize the unique demands of each dimension. The well-functioning planning process deals with all these objectives. In this chapter and the next, we will address planning in the two-dimensional matrix (Chapter Ten) and in the more complex designs (Chapter Eleven).

Goal Alignment, Dispute Resolution, and Coordination Mechanisms

In addition to employing the communication processes described in Chapter Nine, effective matrix organizations use a connected system of team decision processes. The joint goal-setting process, for example, takes place in the context of the planning process for the organization in which the matrix is embedded. The planning process aligns goals throughout the organization and across the various dimensions of the structure. Let us use the national account example again to illustrate these processes.

The plans for national accounts are generated by the national account teams. The plans for the regions are generated by the regional teams. The planning process for the national sales organization as a whole entails reconciling and aligning the two teams representing the two sides of the sales organization. The two-boss managers are key links between the two sides in the alignment process. The entire process is driven by the top team led by the national sales manager.

For the planning process to function effectively, it needs to be supported by a multidimensional information system. That is, revenues and costs must be recorded and collected to show national accounts' revenues and costs as well as regional revenues and costs. Recall that it is essential that both sides of the matrix use the same information. When ABB was created by a merger of Asea from Sweden and Brown Boveri of Switzerland, the first act of the CEO, Percy Barnevik, was to assemble a team of a dozen people. They were to create a new IT and accounting system for managing the business-country matrix. It took them nine months. In the end they rolled out the ABACUS system, which was used by everyone at ABB. Barnevik established a common accounting language (ABACUS) and a common spoken and written language, which he said was "broken English."

The planning process usually starts with the issuance of guidelines from the top team. These guidelines set expectations, indicate the rates of interest and inflation to be used, and contain forecasts for the industry and the economy. The regional and national account teams each take off from the guidelines. The national accounts team consists of the regional national account managers (RNAMs) from each region in which the customer is active. The national account managers then lead the team through the development of a long-term strategy and short-term plan for the account. The result will be targets for long- and short-term revenue, growth, margins, share of customer spending, customer satisfaction, and whatever other goals are useful.

The regional team develops the same strategies and plans for their local regional accounts. The regional team then adds in the national accounts to their local accounts to get a total region plan. If there is a mismatch between the initial region plan and the initial national account plan, the RNAMs play a facilitating role. A face-to-face meeting with the RNAM, the national account manager, and the region manager may be necessary to reach an agreement. It is in these dialogues that the RNAM represents the region in the national account team and the national account in the regional team. The process, when it becomes part of the normal way of operating, usually leads to agreement. Initially in a new matrix there may be more disagreement than usual, but these issues are expected and will require leadership attention during implementation. Figure 10.1 represents the two sales teams with the RNAMs as the interface between them.

The top team consists of the regional sales managers and the national account managers and is led by the national sales

Figure 10.1: Sales Teams with Regional National Account Managers (RNAMs) as the Links

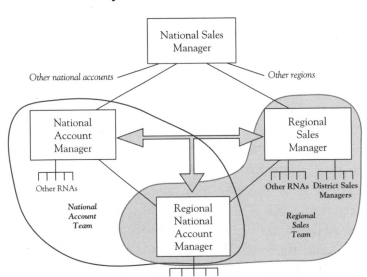

manager. This group becomes the court of appeals for settling disputes between the two sides of the matrix. The process works best when differences are quickly escalated to the top team. Needless to say, the process works best when the top group acts like a team. Part of the leader's task is to set the expectation that disputes are a natural consequence of using a matrix organization. For example, the company may want to grow customer share and volume in the national accounts. The company may also need to show improved profits and margins to Wall Street. It is very likely that in some regions, local accounts are more profitable and show better margins. So it is quite natural to have disputes over where to invest in additional sales efforts in a region. It is up to the teams to debate and problem-solve to reach a solution. One scenario might be that national account I is an enterprise account and gets special attention. So the region may decide that it will invest in national account I to grow share, but not invest in national accounts II and III. Instead the region will invest in the most profitable local accounts to boost this year's profit performance. National account managers II and III may want to discuss this decision with the top team. The debate would then revolve around the company's current financial situation, competitive threats at accounts II and III, and the consequences of not growing customer share. In the process, team members may generate and discuss other alternatives. In the end, the team reaches consensus, or the national sales manager, who is ultimately responsible, will decide. The national account managers for national accounts II and III would have their goals adjusted accordingly.

The entire process of communication and team planning is represented in Figure 10.2. It shows that all the processes are linked. These processes are the coordination mechanisms and represent the costs of managing the interdependence between regions and national accounts. Recall that this interdependence arises because the company wants to service both national and local accounts. Some of the time these objectives will conflict,

Figure 10.2: The Top Team Manages the Linked System of Coordination Mechanisms

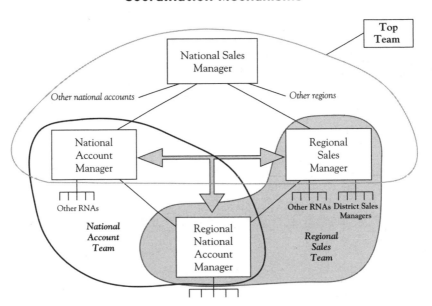

and the team compositions shown in Figure 10.2 are intended to resolve these conflicts in the interest of the company and in a timely manner.

A tool that is useful in this planning process is a spreadsheet that links the regional and account plans. A planning spreadsheet is shown in Figure 10.3. It is another way to represent the interdependencies. The cells at the intersections of the rows and columns represent the RNAM roles where goals need to be aligned. Along the sides of the spreadsheet are the two sides of the matrix.

The regions are represented by the rows. The national and local accounts are represented by the columns. In the planning process, the regional sales teams complete a regional plan with goals for each national account in the region and their local accounts. Each regional team completes a row on the spreadsheet. Each national account team completes a plan for a column. Each column contains cells for the goals for that national

Figure 10.3: Spreadsheet Planning Tool

Top Team

National Sales Manager	National Account I	National Account II	National Account III	Local Accounts	Total Region
Western Region	Shared goals	Shared goals	Shared goals	Shared goals	Total Western Region
Central Region	Shared goals	Shared goals	Shared goals	Shared goals	Total Central Region
Eastern Region	Shared goals	Shared goals	Shared goals	Shared goals	Total Eastern Region
	Total Account I	Total Account II	Total Account III	Total Local	Total National

Shared goals for revenue, growth, customer share, and customer satisfaction

account in each region. Each cell on the sheet represents an RNAM who is responsible for meeting the goals in the cell. These goals usually relate to revenue, margins, growth, and customer share. All of the actors in this discussion must reach agreement on the specific goals for each cell, which then drive the total sales projections. This team-based planning process aligns the goals for the regions and for the national accounts. The regions and national accounts have the same goals, indicated in the figure as shared goals. The region and the national account are jointly accountable to meet those goals. But in reality it is the RNAMs who are accountable, and both sides of the matrix are expected to support them. The totals for the regions add up to the total for national sales, as do the totals for the national and local accounts. In the process, sales are double-counted in the regions and the national account figures. This convention avoids nonproductive disputes about dividing the credit between the two sides of the matrix. The finance group later eliminates the dual counting for the total. The total represents the commitment that the national sales manager makes to the company.

The spreadsheet becomes the scorecard and management tool used by the national sales manager. Of course, no sooner is agreement obtained for the planning period than customers begin to change their orders. The spreadsheets often turn into dashboards employing the red, yellow, and green system. The national sales leader and the top team can review the red accounts each week. At these times, they may shift resources to an RNAM or a district. They may accept the reality of an underperformer for the period and have a couple of the green accounts make up the shortfall. Thus the spreadsheet is a useful tool for visually representing the complete national situation, for gaining agreement on the plan, and for managing the fulfillment of that plan.

The spreadsheet is also useful as a link to the performance management system and the reward system. The cells in the spreadsheet are the goals to be met. Each side of the matrix is

Figure 10.4: Spreadsheet for the Western Sales Region

	National Account I	National Account II	National Account III	Regional Account I	Regional Account II	Local Accounts	District Totals
District A							
District B							
District C							
District D							
District E							
Account Totals							Regional Total

then expected to try to meet all its goals. That is, a national account manager and the national account team try to meet the goals for each region. The regional manager and the regional team try to meet all their account goals, national and local. The RNAMs are accountable for the goals contained in their cell. So the planning and goal-setting processes matter. They directly relate to the measurement and rewarding of performance.

The same process can be put in place within a region. Figure 10.4 shows a spreadsheet for the western region. It shows the national and local accounts as columns; it also shows that there are two regional accounts that span the districts, which make up the rows. The western region can be managed using the same processes as those that are used at national level. In this way, the company can observe early in people's careers who can shine using matrix structures and processes.

Summary

In this chapter, we have seen how the linked teams prepare the plans that align goals and facilitate performance measurement across the matrix. The national account teams and the regional teams are linked by the RNAMs, who participate in both. The national account teams and the regional sales teams are linked to the top team through the common membership of the national accounts managers and the regional sales managers. The processes for managing a matrix are very much team based. The entire system is guided by the spreadsheet planning process. The spreadsheet becomes the tool for managing the outcomes of the process and keeping the goals aligned.

11

PLANNING PROCESSES IN THE COMPLEX MATRIX

In Chapter Ten, we looked at the planning and resource allocation processes for the two-dimensional matrix. In this chapter, we address the more complex matrix models. Aligning goals, resolving conflict, and setting priorities are even more important in these designs. In addition to discussing the planning process, in this chapter I describe the large-scale meeting, which involves hundreds of people, and the jam, which can involve thousands. These processes are used to get timely decisions from large numbers of people and to reach out to all who are impacted in these complex forms.

What About Complex Matrix Designs?

The examples given in Chapter Ten used simple matrix structures. Discussing the simple structure aids in the understanding of the concepts, but in reality, most matrix designs are complex, in terms of both levels and dimensions. Of necessity, companies employ more complex communication patterns across the matrix, more complex spreadsheets, and more complex IT infrastructures and accounting systems to support the matrix structure. Further, they use more complex team designs. All these capabilities are then pulled together in the overall planning process.

Multiple Levels

A complex matrix arises when there are two or more levels between the two-boss manager and the leader. In this case, communication is desired between both sets of peers. The key link remains the one at the level above the two-boss manager. One planning spreadsheet is used at the top of the matrix and a more detailed one at the bottom. These spreadsheets are like those at the national sales level and at the regional level, respectively (see Figures 10.3 and 10.4). A more critical issue arises, however, because the teams are no longer linked. The companies that are effective at matrix have worked out a number of ways for dealing with this issue and for other issues resulting from multidimensional matrix designs.

Degussa Catalytic Converters (DCC) is a good example. DCC is a single business unit that was spun off from Degussa, the German chemical company. DCC's products are the catalytic converters that go into automobile exhaust systems to reduce undesirable emissions and pollution. Each product is customized for an engine and a customer, such as Volkswagen or BMW. DCC, being a single business, is organized as a regional-functional matrix organization. The structure is shown in Figure 11.1. The salespeople report directly to the regional manager. The other functions are matrixed. However, most of the activity takes place

Figure 11.1: Degussa Catalytic Converters'
Regional-Functional Matrix Structure

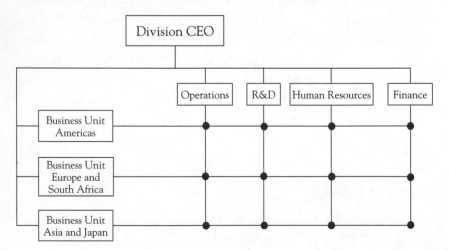

in cross-functional customer teams. These teams direct several cross-functional project teams developing new products for new engines and improving old ones. The BMW team, for example, prepares the long-range plan and short-term budget for the total customer relationship with BMW. The team coordinates and prioritizes projects for the new engines for the 3 Series and 5 Series. A product improvement project for the 7 Series rounds out the product development portfolio.

A customer team for BMW is shown in Figure 11.2. It is a cross-functional and cross-country team. The team is most active in BMW's home country, where most of the product development work is done. It is chaired by the representative from applied technology because the technical development requirements are high. Some of the other customer teams, such as the one for Volkswagen, are led by the sales and marketing representative. The leadership of the teams varies depending on the customer requirements. In addition to the product development plan, the team prepares the next year's budget for revenue and costs from all countries and regions and all functions. Thus the customer plans are by function and by country and region. These plans are reviewed by the top team, which consists of the

Figure 11.2: BMW Customer Team

	Brazil	Germany	North America	China
Marketing and Sales	X	X	X	X
Applied Technology		LEADER		
R&D		X		
Manufacturing	V	X	V	V
Logistics		X		
Quality		X		

Note: X = member of core team; V = member of extended team

division CEO and his or her direct reports. When the budgets are completed, the functional managers have a spreadsheet showing their commitments by country and by customer. The regional business unit managers can see their commitments by function, by customer, and by country.

There are seven customer teams for the largest seven customers. The top team consists of the functional and business unit leaders who do not lead the customer teams. In order to link to the customer teams, members of the top team are each assigned the oversight of one or two customer teams. They attend important team meetings, receive the communications from team meetings and activities, and talk frequently with the customer team leader as well as the customer. The top team member provides counsel to the customer team when it prepares its plans and budgets. He or she helps the customer teams prepare for budget reviews conducted by the top team. In this way, the top team overseer stays informed about the day-to-day business issues that the customer team is addressing. The overseer is the link between the customer teams and the top team. If a cross-functional dispute arises that the customer team cannot resolve, the overseer and the customer team leader take the issue to the top team for discussion and resolution. The overseer is prepared to present and discuss the issue. The top team meets for a full day once a month for reviews of teams and to deal with issues that are escalated to them. Thus the assignment of overseer roles is one way that companies forge the link between the top team and the teams at the working level.

Complex Spreadsheets

In the cases of multidimensional matrix structures, the spreadsheets become difficult to represent in two-dimensional form. Sometimes a series of two-dimensional spreadsheets can be used. For example, let us assume that the company represented in the spreadsheet in Figure 10.3 added a new software product. It is now selling its hardware product line as before but is adding a new software product line. The national sales manager could have a spreadsheet like the one shown in Figure 10.3 for hardware and another one for software. Or all three dimensions could be combined into one spreadsheet, as shown in Figure 11.3. The software product line has been added to each of the four customer columns. Commitments for revenue and margins for the account managers, regional managers, and product managers can be obtained from the spreadsheet. The totals for all managers and the national sales manager can be shown as well.

When there are larger numbers of entries into the spreadsheet, the visual representation of the total picture is impossible. In these cases, the traffic-light system of red, yellow, and green can be useful. The red cells can be called up and their rows and columns displayed. Indeed, at ABB there were five thousand profit centers throughout the world. The top team could call up the red cells or any cells in the ABACUS system for discussion and issue resolution. Thus, as I have noted elsewhere, an important part of the infrastructure to support the decision making in a matrix is the multidimensional accounting system. These accounting systems are both multilevel and multidimensional. Equally important, it is essential for the top team to have both access to a high-level representation of the total situation and the ability to drill down and examine the issues at the intersections of the matrix.

Complex Teams

The other issue that arises with the multidimensional matrix is the design of teams for each dimension and the linkages between these teams. In the example in Chapter Ten, we saw teams for customers (national accounts) and regions. At DCC we saw a structure for customers, functions, and regions. For P&G or Citibank, however, we need teams for customers, countries, product lines, and functions. Each of these teams

Figure 11.3: National Sales Spreadsheet by Product (H/W and S/W), by Accounts, and by Region

	National Account I		National Account II		National Account III		Local Accounts		Product Regional Totals		Region Totals
	H/W	S/W	H/W	S/W	H/W	S/W	H/W	S/W			
Western Region									H/W		
									S/W		
Central Region									H/W		
									S/W		
Eastern Region									H/W		
									S/W		
Product Account Totals									National H/W Total		NATIONAL TOTAL
Account Totals									National S/W Total		

will then prepare a plan for its row or column on the planning spreadsheet. Let us look at the design of complex team structures (see also Galbraith, 2002, chap. 5).

Core Team, Extended Team One approach to complex team design is to use a core team and an extended team. This design was used by Citibank when it began to form global account teams for customers who wanted to be served by one team at a single interface. Citibank's team for Nestlé was chaired by the global account manager, who served Nestlé's CFO in Vevey, Switzerland. A core team was formed by account managers who served Nestlé full-time in the global financial centers—New York, London, Frankfurt, Hong Kong, and Tokyo. The extended team was the core team plus the account managers who served Nestlé in fifty-four countries where Nestlé needed financial support and service. Also on the core team were product managers from high-volume product units and representatives from the finance and risk management functions. Citibank's lead product for global customers is cash management. Citi is present in more countries than any other bank and is positioned to manage a multinational's cash better than competitors. So a cash management product manager and a treasury products manager for foreign exchange and derivatives are members of the core team. They could be joined by another product manager from Asian debt products if Nestlé were undertaking a financing initiative in China. Other product lines and functions are represented on the extended team. So the team consists of salespeople from different countries, specialists from the product lines, and functional experts.

The core team prepares the Nestlé strategic plan and sets the profit and revenue goals for the planning period. As the period unfolds, the core team interacts daily and holds a weekly phone call and a monthly meeting. Members of the core team are assigned to be contacts for the members of the extended team. The extended team is canvassed for input prior to the preparation of the plan and are asked to comment on and improve the final plan. The core team member holds a weekly conversation with the members of the extended team in his or her region. The entire core plus extended team has a monthly phone call or audio conference. These monthly conferences are well planned, and someone in strategic planning facilitates them. The purpose of the conferences is to review performance of the customer team by region and product using the appropriate spreadsheet. New initiatives are reviewed and issues are raised for discussion. In this way, Citibank links its customer teams with the countries, products, and functions making up the structure.

Multidimensional Teams Procter & Gamble has also created global customer teams for Wal-Mart, Tesco, Carrefour, Metro, Ahold, and a few others. These global retailers are accounting for an increasing percentage of P&G's sales. Whereas Citibank now has around seventeen hundred teams and global customers, P&G has about ten. The company started with Wal-Mart in North America. Initially it created sales teams that represented all of P&G's products that were sold to Wal-Mart. Then the national account team was expanded to create a supply chain partnership. There was a cross-functional team for each product category. Today these categories are called global business units (GBUs). At first, there were about eighty people located in Fayetteville, Arkansas, dedicated to the Wal-Mart account. As Wal-Mart and the other global retailers expanded internationally, the teams grew to incorporate the geographic dimension. The team for Wal-Mart is now about 250 people. There are small teams of ten or twelve in each country where Wal-Mart is present. These teams report to the global account unit in Arkansas. A partial organization of the global Wal-Mart account team is shown in Figure 11.4. Each country is a cross-functional and cross-GBU team. Each representative reports to his or her function, GBU, and country manager as well as to the

Figure 11.4: A Portion of the Global Wal-Mart Team at Procter & Gamble

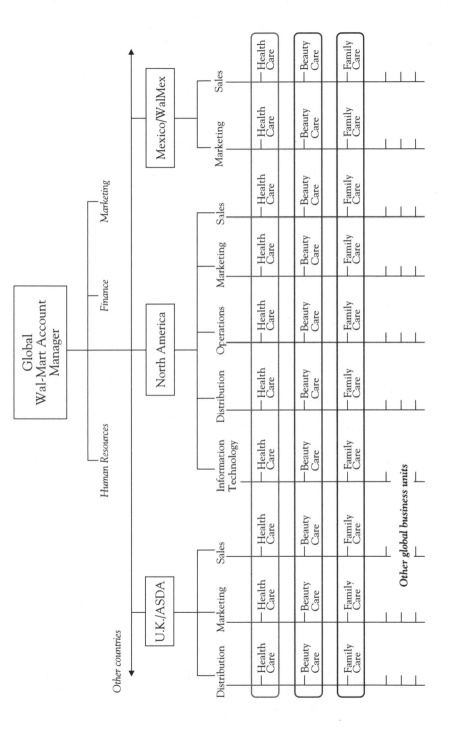

global customer account. Each customer country team prepares a plan and budget for each business unit and function serving the customer in the country. These country plans are combined into a global plan that is documented by business, function, and country. Thus, for the top global retailers, P&G has customer teams that are cross functional, cross GBU, and cross country.

As noted elsewhere, many companies with complex matrix structures use the planning process to provide forums for integrating the multiple-matrix dimensions. The linked teams for customers, products, countries, and functions prepare plans for the period. Goal alignment is sought through communication between the different sides of the matrix within the team structures, supported by the spreadsheet tool and the IT infrastructure. Then the official plan usually results from a review process or a conference of the participants. These capstone events are themselves well planned and orchestrated. Intel is a good example of one of the companies that follow such extensive planning processes.

Matrix Planning Process—Intel Example In the 1980s, Intel created a strategic staff unit whose task was to manage the strategic planning process, which I have described here as the spreadsheet goal alignment process. The leader of the unit was Les Vadsz, who was a member of the executive staff that was run by Andy Grove. Through Vadsz's participation in staff meetings and conversations with the members of the management team, he was aware of the thinking of Intel's leadership. He and his staff also attended the team planning meetings of the businesses and the functions. These were the two dominant dimensions of the matrix, and each had teams whose plans were reviewed. Through these meetings, the strategic staff had a good idea of the issues to be addressed in the planning reviews. The head of strategic staff and the heads of the businesses and functions would agree on the five issues that would be the best use of everyone's time in the review meetings.

Strategic staff would prepare the agenda for the reviews and send out the materials to be read. The staff would facilitate the review itself. There was very little presentation and a lot of discussion and debate about the issues. One of the unique features of the review was that anyone could attend, either in person or by phone. In this way, all the other dimensions of the matrix could listen and contribute if needed. The attendees could not just be devil's advocates at these reviews—that would be too easy. The leaders would often challenge the devil's advocates and ask them for their solution to the issue that they were critiquing. The norm was to behave responsibly. The discussions and debates were often heated. Some decisions would be made and others tabled for the executive staff meeting after the reviews. Some others would be assigned to a team of four or five people, who would analyze the issue and make a proposal. These decisions were recorded by the strategic staff, and the results of this final meeting were communicated to all parties.

In summary, the Intel planning process is intelligently designed, the high-priority and tough issues are escalated and placed front and center, materials are read ahead of time with a minimum amount of time spent on presentation, everyone who needs to know and contribute can attend, the issues get the heated discussion they deserve, and the tough issues get resolved. These reviews have been a disciplined process at Intel.

Matrix Planning Process—Japanese Company Example In contrast to Intel's model, some Japanese companies use a conference model. The top 150 or so managers go to Japan for about ten days of meetings. The meetings are called "Sony days" or, at Canon, "summit meetings." At these meetings, the businesses can discuss their cross-country and cross-functional issues, the regions can discuss their cross-business and cross-functional issues, and the functions can discuss their cross-country and cross-business issues. Each dimension can address all the rows and columns in the spreadsheet. For a morning meeting at the summit, Canon can have the western European region meet the copier business in meeting room A and the North American region meet with the digital camera business in meeting room B. The next morning, the businesses switch rooms and repeat the process. The real business, of course, gets done at night, Japanese style. The summit provides for conversations between all the sides of the matrix in a facilitated and supportive environment. By the final day, the decisions have been made and all the cells on the spreadsheet filled in.

Get the System in a Room

A number of techniques and approaches are evolving that can provide more management processes for aligning the different dimensions of the multidimensional matrix structures. Many of these stem from Marv Weisbord's idea that to solve some problems, one needs to get all the key players in a room and work the issue through to a resolution. He called this idea "Get the system in a room." The system of key players could be 17 people, 51, or 137. It does not matter how many people are essential to the resolution. What is important is to get them all together and work with them until the issue is resolved.

The reason I am spending time on this subject is that the large-scale meeting (also known as large group intervention) is ideal for the complex matrix organization. The complex matrix with three or more dimensions generates a great deal of conflict. The number of key players who have the information relevant to the conflicts and who need to commit to shared goals can be around 100 to 150 people. The CEOs and the few corporate leaders cannot always make the Solomon-like judgments to break the ties. Getting the system in a room is a good answer to resolving these conflicts.

Of course the facilitators of these sessions need to be extremely skilled to manage groups of this size. But today there are people who can do this. Marv Weisbord and his colleague Sandra

Janoff are two of them. They have created Future Search—The Network, a Web site for exchanging ideas and matching clients with people who can run large-scale meetings. You can find them at http://futuresearch.net. Billie Albans and Barbara Bunker have run these large-scale meetings for years. Their book on the subject (Bunker and Albans, 1997) has been well received and is a good guide to the topic. I have worked with Stu Winby on these issues. During the HP-Compaq merger, Stu ran "decision accelerators" (DAs) when decisions were needed but people were encountering impasses. The DAs are Stu's version of the large-scale meetings in which the system of key people is gathered in a room. Stu and his team facilitate contentious discussions during the course of one or two days to arrive at a series of decisions. DAs can be used, for example, in finalizing the plan and budget during an intensive and particularly complex spreadsheet planning process. You can find Stu at www.innovation-point.com.

There are numerous times during the year when the large group meeting can be useful. Matrix organizations generate their share of conflicts and impasses. It is desirable to resolve these issues quickly and completely. The reality of matrix organizations is often the opposite, however. So what happens when strategic conflicts are not raised or are raised but not resolved? What happens is that problems fall to lower levels until someone is forced to make a decision.

Let's look at an example from a pharmaceutical company. The head of clinical trials in France was experiencing a conflict between his two bosses. The head of global clinical trials wanted to increase the number of trials being conducted in France. There were several well-known physicians in France. Her thinking was that if these physicians successfully conducted the trials, their participation and advocacy would add to the credibility of the company's promotion of the approved drugs. The other boss of the head of clinical trials was the French country manager. The country manager wanted fewer clinical trials in France. The expense of conducting more trials would raise his costs. And the French country manager knew that the executive vice president of Europe position was going to be open in the next year. So the country manager, seeing himself as a candidate for the job, wanted his numbers to be especially good this year. As a result of these conflicting interests, the two bosses could not agree. To make matters worse, the leadership did not act to resolve the issue either.

The result was that the decision fell to the head of clinical trials in France. When he arrived at the office on Monday morning, he had to decide what to do. He did not have the option of not deciding. If he did nothing, he had in effect decided with the country manager not to increase the number of trials. Or he might seek some sort of compromise with a small increase in the number of trials. But the point is that he had to decide.

Thus organizational problems in matrix companies cascade. They are the opposite of "the buck stops here" leadership. If leaders fail to resolve conflicts, the conflict does not disappear. It falls to someone at a lower level, who must act on Monday morning. The result is that strategic decisions are delegated by default to middle managers who usually do not have the training or the perspective to make them, and the same issue could be decided in different ways by the different managers, which leads to inconsistency in the organization. So how do we handle these issues?

Resolving strategic conflicts is clearly a leadership responsibility. The conflict in the pharmaceutical company example could be handled simply by having the CEO call the two bosses into the office, shut the door, and say, "We're not leaving here until the issue is resolved." Or the leadership could see a bigger issue, which they did in this case. This conflict is between clinical trials and France. Tomorrow it could be a conflict with Japan or the United Kingdom. How does the company resolve this issue and put in place a process to resolve similar issues in the future? These activities require that the company get the system in a room. The leaders, therefore, convened a large group meeting. The players were key country managers, finance functional managers, experts in new product development, and the key clinical trials managers.

After conducting the two-day session, the pharmaceutical company had established a new funding process for clinical trials. The country managers would fund trials for products unique to their country; global clinical trials managers would fund new global products. The global unit would get a budget that they could use to fund trials in countries of the global unit's choosing. The funds would be booked as revenue for the receiving country. The countries would then compete for these funds along with third-party companies to whom the trials could be outsourced. The new process is a significant improvement to the delegation-by-default process.

In all cases, the resolution of these national conflicts is the responsibility of the leadership. The large-scale meeting or the DAs are powerful tools for dealing with conflicts and nonaligned goals, whether they are disputes about budget or about filling in the cells of the multidimensional spreadsheets. These processes are extremely useful. One can imagine a unit like Intel's strategic staff that has the responsibility to find these strategic conflicts and conduct the DAs to resolve them. In this way, the company would not rely on voluntary escalation processes, which may cover up issues or raise them too slowly.

Online Processes

Large group meetings with as many as two thousand people have been convened, but to engage larger numbers and at a lower cost, a new process, called a jam, is emerging. A jam is a process invented at IBM for conducting "conversations" in large organizations around a top-priority issue, with the intent being to build a consensus around actionable ideas (Spangler, Kreulen, and Newswanger, 2006). It is based on "getting the system on a portal" or the intranet. It is more organized than a chat room.

"A jam is typically organized into a handful of separate 'forums' (from 4 to 7) each on a different topic related to the overall Jam topic. The Jam is continuous and for a limited time period (usually between 48 and 72 hours). During the event participants can come and go into the Jam as often as they like. Participants who register at the site can make original posts or reply to existing posts" (p. 3).

As the jam proceeds, the conversations are monitored by moderators who are assigned to the various forums. The streams of thought are also analyzed by Jamalyzer, data-mining software for unstructured text. Themes are extracted and posted, as are hot topics. The postings and summaries can be searched by topic or by participant. Postings and summaries can be e-mailed to solicit input from key individuals. So the discussion is facilitated and summarized at twelve-hour intervals. The facilitators and management can create a final summary and a list of actions that will result from the jam. Let's look at an example from IBM (Hemp and Stewart, 2004).

Sam Palmisano took over in 2002 as the CEO of IBM. He felt that although IBM had set financial goals to shoot for, the company needed some values that indicated what it stood for. The founder, Thomas Watson, had set three "Basic Beliefs" about a hundred years ago, and Palmisano felt that they needed to be brought up-to-date. He wanted a new set of values to energize the company and to serve as a common set of guidelines to steer decisions day in and day out in IBM's complex matrix. He used a jam, called Values Jam, to establish a new set of values.

Palmisano first laid the groundwork for the effort. At a meeting of the top three hundred managers, he raised the issue of creating new values. He tossed out four ideas—respect, customer, excellence, and innovation—to serve as thought starters for the new set. He then expanded the discussion by means of a survey to over a thousand employees. The survey engaged people at all levels and locations. On the basis of this groundwork, three proposed values were set forth for discussion during Values Jam. The proposals were

- Commitment to the customer
- Excellence through innovation
- Integrity that earns trust

The Values Jam took place over three days in July 2003. Over fifty thousand IBMers logged on to the jam and made about ten thousand postings. Facilitators and the Jamalyzer pored over the postings during and after the session. Then a small team, including Palmisano, summarized and stated the new company values:

- Dedication to every client's success
- Innovation that matters—for our company and for the world
- Trust and personal responsibility in all relationships

These were announced by the CEO over the intranet in November 2003. The published values were accompanied by some explanations and example quotes from the jam. More than two hundred thousand people downloaded the document.

Palmisano then followed through by appointing a business unit manager to head up the effort to implement the values. She and her team identified gaps between the values and IBM's current practices and planned a follow-on jam. The next jam was called LogJam and was dedicated to confirming gaps between IBM's lived values today and the new values. The team also solicited ideas to close those gaps. That jam led to several process changes—for example, changes related to the pricing of multiple–business unit solutions.

IBM has invented an online process for facilitating a conversation among thousands of people around the world. These jams focus on high-priority topics and lead to a reasonable consensus on the issue. Like the decision accelerators, the jams can be used to resolve the inevitable tough conflicts that arise in multidimensional matrix structures.

Summary

In this chapter and the preceding, we looked at the processes that lead to coordinated efforts in multidimensional matrix structures. These processes vary from informal face-to-face discussions to formal performance management processes.

More elaborate management processes for planning and resource allocation are also necessary. The tools to implement these can be two-dimensional spreadsheets or multidimensional representations. The people completing these spreadsheets meet in small groups to prepare the plans and use the large-scale meeting to resolve disagreements. These meetings are techniques for getting the system in a room; in the case of IBM, the jam gets the system on a portal. These sessions use conversations among thousands of people to arrive at an actionable consensus about issues. All these techniques involve the large number of people who are interdependent in today's complex matrix designs.

12

HUMAN RESOURCES POLICIES

The human resources (HR) policies, collectively, are some of the most powerful design shapers of the successful matrix organization. The design of policies for recruiting, socialization, development, promotion, rotation, performance management, and rewarding all need to form a matrix-supporting package. That is, they need to be aligned, just as do all the other policies constituting the Star Model as a whole. These policies are central to the creating of the human capital, social capital, reward systems, and culture that underlie an effectively functioning matrix organization.

Some of the best models for an integrated package of HR practices are found in professional services firms (Maister, 1985; Eccles and Crane, 1988; Lorsch, 2001; Lorsch and Tierney, 2002; Maister and Walker, 2006). Professionals have always worked under circumstances that require a matrix organization. Professionals are highly specialized but must come together in multidisciplinary teams for projects or customer engagements. The early matrix designs, as you will recall, came out of R&D labs. But investment banks, consulting firms, and big law firms all operate under similar conditions. All have become global and multidimensional matrix organizations. In particular, the one-firm firms, wherein people think and act as if they come from a single firm no matter how diverse it is, have created the policies that other companies can also use to support their multidimensional matrix organizations. These "one-firm firms place great emphasis on firm-wide coordination of decision making, group identity, cooperative teamwork and institutional commitment" (Maister, 1985, p. 4). These are exactly the same attributes that support a matrix organization. Let us start by examining the policies that create the human capital that is necessary to facilitate matrix structures.

Human Capital

Human capital is the sum total of the skills, competencies, and experiences of all the people who make up the firm. Leaders can increase the firm's human capital by making the company attractive to talent, investing in recruiting and selection, and delivering developmental experiences to its managers. Although every firm says that human capital is important and every firm performs these tasks, it is the top-performing matrix organizations that excel at them. The reason they excel at human capital building is that their leaders invest enormous amounts of time in recruiting, assessing talent, and developing management. As Lorsch and Tierney put it, "In great firms . . . the senior people worry as much about missing out on or losing new talent as they do about missing out on or losing good clients" (p. 66). These firms know that in the short run, performance is based on the people who pay them (customers), but that in the long run, performance is based on the people whom they pay (their talent).

Whom to Attract, Recruit, and Select

The first step in the process is to know what kinds of people to seek to have join your organization. Like other companies, matrix organizations seek qualified people, but in particular they want people who will thrive in a matrix organization. Usually these are people who can influence without authority, who are naturally collaborative, who like to be part of something important, and who are capable of building high-trust relationships and interpersonal networks. Choosing suitable people for a matrix organization also means saying no to solo flyers, those who are very entrepreneurial, who like to do their own thing and have a need to control and be independent. These people will not fit. At Goldman Sachs they say, "You learn from day one around here that we gang-tackle problems. If your ego won't permit that, you won't be effective here" (Maister, 1985, p. 4).

So recruiting and selection are very much focused on people with a willingness to collaborate and the skills to do so. Some firms even try to capture the idea with an acronym. At Hewitt Associates consulting business, they search for SWANs. That is, they look for people who are smart, who work hard, and who are ambitious and nice. Of course it is the last attribute that is surprising, but for Hewitt "nice" means people who will implement the internal cooperation and teamwork that the business requires.

The Mayo Clinic is one of the best examples of attracting and selecting talent (Berry, 2004). The competitive advantage of Mayo is its integrated multispecialty practice. It assembles a team of experts for patients, delivers the necessary care, then disbands in order to reconfigure to meet the needs of the next patient. To understand Mayo is to understand its processes for building and maintaining its collaborative culture.

First, Mayo relies on self-selection. The clinic has a reputation that it promotes at medical schools. If you are someone who likes independence, covets personal acclaim, is short on interpersonal skills, and wants to make a lot of money, do not apply to the Mayo Clinic. If you see the practice of medicine as best delivered through the integration of a team of specialists working on a salary, Mayo is the place for you. When a candidate arrives and goes through the interview process, he or she will be interviewed by cross-disciplinary interview teams. They believe that if their organization works in teams, then why not interview in teams? The candidate can see the organization in action. Again the candidate can use self-selection. The interview process brings the team culture alive in the presence of the candidate. Candidates can ask themselves, "Is this the way that I would like to work? Am I comfortable in this setting?"

Mayo also invests significant resources in the selection process. It has studied and determined what kind of people will thrive in its collaborative culture. It wants to appeal to those people who have a high commitment to patient care, and turns away hard workers with a strong attachment to extrinsic rewards. Mayo focuses the selectivity on personality traits and dimensions of character. These are attributes that are unlikely to change easily and that are critical to the maintenance of Mayo's collaborative culture. The clinic then invests in a time-consuming and collaborative hiring process to select those who will thrive. As already mentioned, candidates are interviewed by groups. Mayo's approach is to involve a lot of people so as to gain good insights into the applicants. In addition, the clinic uses behavioral interviewing techniques to determine a candidate's values. The candidates are asked to describe projects on which they have worked and accomplishments of which they are proud. If the candidate uses a lot of "I's" rather than "we's," he is not hired. "A superstar for us is someone who knows how to bring a team together" (quoted in Berry, 2004, p. 232).

Mayo also has very strict hiring standards, and it maintains them. For example, nurses at the clinic describe how surprised they were at the rigorous hiring process. They had thought that with a shortage of qualified nurses, they would automatically and easily be hired. But instead they went through multiple group interviews and were peppered with all kinds of questions. Some did not make it. The fit between the personality of new hires and the collaborative culture is rigorously maintained. The process itself communicates to the candidates. If so much time and effort are invested in hiring the right people, the company must really value its human resources. The people also feel special having survived a tough process and are more likely to feel committed to the organization.

The physicians sometimes are observed for a longer period of time than other personnel. Some physicians are hired from outside and go through the process I've described. But Mayo's preferred way of hiring physicians is to observe and work with them as interns and residents for a few years. In this way, the clinic can see the future physicians in action and get a very good idea of their natural style of behavior. Still other physicians may be the product of the small (forty-person) medical school that Mayo operates. Thus many of the physicians at the Mayo Clinic have been rather thoroughly acculturated in the Mayo way. To be selected as a student or intern, the physician still needs to go through the selection process.

The use of interns is also popular among professional services companies. The internships allow both self-selection on the part of the intern and informed selection for the company. There is nothing quite like working side by side for getting to know a person and a company. General Electric is another user of interns. A number of engineers join GE through this route (Bartlett and McLean, 2004).

Not all companies have the attractive reputation of the Mayo Clinic and the attractive mission of the health care industry. These companies have to spend more time and effort recruiting the talent from which they can select. Indeed, today it is suggested that the power has shifted away from companies and toward the talent. It is the talented people who also select companies. The current situation has been described as "the War for Talent" (Michaels, Handfield-Jones, and Axelrod, 2001). This situation certainly applies to recruiting talent for matrix organizations. Every company wants its version of SWANs.

As we have already discussed, top-performing companies work to determine who will thrive in their matrix organization. They work equally hard to develop an employee value proposition (EVP) that appeals to that type of person. Just as they work hard to gather customer insights and learn what their customers want, top-performing companies also develop employee insights and learn what their type of prospective candidates want from an employer.

The EVP is what employees actually experience and receive from the company. It should not be padded with high-sounding words but portray the company honestly and realistically so that people can self-select as well as be attracted. Matrix organizations can provide attractive opportunities for people who want to work in multinational organizations and who like to work in multicultural teams, engage in rotational assignments, and work in a growth company. In addition to being realistic and appealing, an EVP may require changes in how the company actually manages and develops its people. These changes usually move a company to a more employee-centric position, because the EVP must provide an advantage over the EVPs of companies competing for the same people who thrive in matrix organizations.

Then the company has to work at getting its EVP across and finding people to whom it will be appealing. The most effective firms apply the strategic mind-set behind their customer value proposition to their EVP. They think in the same competitive terms of employee proposition advantage. They think about where to find the people they want and then work hard to recruit them. From this strategic view of recruiting, several best practices have emerged.

Search for Talent Continuously In the old recruitment model, the company searched for a person when a position became available. This approach assumes that people are readily available. But what are the chances that a talented person is looking for your kind of position at the exact time when it is available? Instead, top companies are always looking for the kind of person they need, whether a position is available or not.

Those companies that work the hardest never miss an opportunity to recruit their versions of the right talent. In normal business dealings with their bank, ad agency, accounting firm, suppliers, and so on, they are searching for talent. At trade shows, they visit all the booths, not just for competitive intelligence, but to discover talent working in the booths. Usually these talented people are not looking for another opportunity at the time, so the searching firms create a database of future candidates, keep in touch, and make offers when the people start to look for new opportunities.

Search in Lots of Diverse Places Companies used to recruit at a standard set of schools. Today they cast a much wider net. Microsoft, for example, starts its process by looking at the resumes of all twenty thousand or so computer science graduates in the United States. It has now extended its search around the world. But Microsoft is not the only company looking worldwide and in unconventional places for talent. The global search for talent is driven by a desire to hire first for cultural fit (rather than just technical expertise). The policy now is to hire for attitude and train for skills for many positions. For example, McKinsey talks to all the White House Fellows each year. These are successful young people who have worked on projects in the White House for a year. While they are away from their past work, McKinsey tries to present them with an opportunity for a second career in consulting. As a matter of fact, McKinsey will recruit anywhere where it can find "natural athletes," its type of smart people or SWANs.

Recruiting Is Everyone's Job In the old recruiting model, the task was delegated to the recruiting department. It ran the process until the final candidates were put in front of the hiring manager. Today companies want everyone to be a talent scout. Drawing from personal referrals from existing employees is one of the most effective recruiting tools there is when current employees are satisfied. So companies are encouraging their current talent to use their networks to recruit new talent. Some companies, such as DoubleClick, offer incentives of up to $1,000 per recruit who joins and stays for at least a year.

The professional services companies again show the way. Lorsch and Tierney (2002, p. 81) found that at the outstanding firms, the leaders were heavily involved in recruiting. Certainly some initial screening was done, but then the partners took over. These firms found that partners were more convincing when presenting the firm to candidates. The partners are also representatives of the firm's culture. Candidates can decide if they want to be like these people. They can ask, "Would I want to work with or for this person?" The partners can also ask similar questions. The process helps both sides determine whether there is a fit or not. So the firms and partners work hard to find the right talent and make themselves attractive to that talent.

In summary, the first step in building the human capital that will thrive in a matrix organization is the recruiting and selection process. The top-performing firms are those that first do the work to identify what type of people will do well in their matrix. They develop an attractive EVP to appeal to these people, and ensure that their management practices deliver it. They develop a hiring profile to select candidates. And, just as important, they search widely and continuously to find their ideal types. Then, once important candidates have been found, the leadership participates actively in the attracting and hiring process. The firms that succeed at attracting and hiring their SWANs are the ones that have worked the hardest at recruiting them.

Developing and Growing the Talent

Once the talent that will potentially thrive in matrix organizations has been hired, the top firms provide the development opportunities these people want. Regardless of how much time and effort were devoted to recruiting, new hires rarely arrive fully developed. The top firms therefore provide opportunities through job experiences to grow these people who will be their future leaders in the matrix. This development process is no different in a matrix organization than in any other type; it is just that the behaviors to be learned and developed are those needed in a matrix.

Normal Development The top professional services companies are again the ones that set the standard on the development dimension. Like other companies, they have learned that development occurs on the job. They arrange challenging assignments and encourage leaders to give candid feedback and coaching. In addition, assessments are made at least every six months. Assessment data are collected from leaders, customers, and everyone with whom the person has worked. The person also gets a candid appraisal every six months. These companies have developed norms whereby people take the time to collect and give assessments, and take talent development seriously. Partners are assessed on several dimensions, one of which is their ability to develop talent. Thus, as they do in their approach to recruiting, the professional services companies invest time and effort in talent development.

Rotational Assignments One of the most important developmental features of the matrix is the use of rotational assignments. As we have seen, matrix structures give rise to conflict between the sides, yet cooperation is critical. If people have held positions on both sides of the matrix, they will have gained experience with both sides of these inevitable conflicts and will thus approach them in an informed, problem-solving manner. A second benefit of rotational assignments is that they foster the creation of a "matrix in people's minds" (Bartlett and Ghoshal, 1990). That is, people behave effectively in a matrix when they understand the whole matrix and the location of key interfaces. Spending time in some different parts of the matrix gives people this total perspective.

Companies have developed a number of different ways of offering rotational assignments. Some, like American Express International, want new managerial hires to see different regions and businesses. A new hire in Europe will spend the first six months in Europe. Then she spends six months in Asia and six months in the Americas. At that point she can choose where to go for her first assignment.

Some companies have a systematic rotation program. Chemical companies hire chemical engineers and start them in R&D. Then the engineers follow the new product that they worked on in R&D into scale-up, manufacturing, and marketing or sales. Thus they enjoy the stability of working with the same new product while also facing the challenge of a new function. The scale-up task is a critical one for the engineer, as it is the first cross-functional challenge. Some engineers take to it and perform well. These people will make good managers, project managers, and cross-functional coordinators. Those engineers who do not excel usually prefer to return to R&D and remain technical specialists. This type of cross-functional experience is very useful in product-function matrix structures.

The aerospace industry systematically rotates managers from functional positions to project management and back again. Project managers are typically engineers. So after running a small engineering group, a high-potential manager runs a small project. If he is successful, the manager runs a larger engineering group and then a larger project. This rotation continues until the manager decides to remain in the function or in project management.

A last example is of a global accounting firm that needs to coordinate global accounts. The challenge is to find people who are experienced with customers and with different geographies, and who have the cooperation skills needed in a matrix organization. These firms have learned to grow their own. An audit firm can serve as an example. A young Swiss auditor was identified as a talented performer on audits of banks in Zurich. When a global team was created for Citibank, the auditor, who had experience in audits of Citibank's subsidiary, became the Swiss representative on the Citibank team. On the basis of his good performance, the auditor agreed to an assignment in the United Kingdom. The move gave the auditor the opportunity to work in the London financial center. While in London, the auditor served as the U.K. representative on the Credit Suisse global team. His next assignment was to lead an in-depth audit of the Credit Suisse First Boston investment bank in the United States. The auditor was then made partner of the audit firm and returned to Zurich. From there he was selected to be the global accounts team leader for Credit Suisse. After several years in the team leader role, the auditor became the global coordinator for the financial services customer segment. The firm assessed the auditor in each assignment for audit performance and knowledge of the financial services industry as usual. But it also assessed his teamwork skills, relationships with customers, ability to influence without authority, cross-cultural skills with customers and team members, and leadership of the cross-border team. Through his experiences and training courses, the auditor was qualified to move into the global coordinator role.

Formal Training and Development The last component of development for managing in a matrix is formal skill training. There are a number of identifiable skills that are needed in matrix organizations; they can be developed in the classroom and small-group simulations. For example, a lot of work in matrix organizations is done in groups or teams. We now know a lot about how groups work. People can be taught how to behave in and lead a problem-solving group. The same can be said about influencing without authority, managing conflict, and building personal networks. The concepts underlying these skills are very teachable, and exercises have been developed that enable people to learn and practice the skills in a safe setting.

A lot of the early failures of matrix organizations can be attributed to the lack of the aforementioned skills and capabilities. There were few people who could influence without authority, few people who had cross-functional experience; there was little capability for working in cross-functional teams, and when faced with the natural conflicts that arose, the teams could not function. We have come a long way since these early days. However, many companies are still weak in managing conflict, especially at the top of the organization and especially in cross-cultural settings.

Some companies have worked to create a culture in which people can effectively confront the natural day-to-day conflicts that arise. General Electric during Jack Welch's tenure developed norms and behaviors for dealing with conflict. Intel is another example. Under Andy Grove's leadership, Intel established norms that support constructive conflict. All managers there go through a course on group problem solving under conditions of conflict. They therefore share a common language for problem solving in the face of conflict. The steps in the process are even posted on the walls of all conference rooms. Thus all managers are equipped with the skill set for dealing with the conflicts that naturally arise in the matrix organization.

In summary, the design of a successful matrix organization requires a set of HR policies for attracting, recruiting, selecting, and developing a population of managers who have the skill sets and mind-sets suitable for collaboration. These HR practices generate the human capital needed to execute a matrix. These managers have the personalities to fit into the matrix organization culture and the skills to facilitate the functioning of the processes that support the matrix. In other words, these HR practices fit with the strategies, structures, and processes of a well-functioning matrix organization.

Reward Systems

The next component of the HR policies to support the matrix is the reward system. Its purpose is to provide the motivation for employees to execute the behaviors that support organizational goals. The formal rewards are promotions, fixed and variable compensation, recognition, and challenging assignments. We will deal primarily with promotions and variable compensation in this section.

The design of the formal reward system must address two components: (1) the types of performance that are needed to support the strategy and the behaviors that underlie that performance, and (2) the performance management process that will generate the information to measure these behaviors and arrive at a full and fair assessment of performance. In a matrix organization, performance is viewed in terms of both objective financial performance and subjective collaborative behaviors. A full and fair process entails collecting information from all the people who are able to observe a person's performance. It also involves an open discussion and analysis of the performance data in order to arrive at a decision for promotion or bonus. Although most companies do not use this kind of full and fair process, many are moving in the right direction. The professional services companies already have implemented this type of assessment process.

What Kinds of Behavior Support the Strategy? The first task is to determine the behaviors that constitute the performance that the company needs. Most firms have four or five categories of behavior against which people are judged for promotion and compensation. At Bain, for example, there are five categories:

1. Client contributions: What have you done to build our relationship with customers or clients?
2. People development: What have you done to recruit and develop the talent for future partners?
3. Knowledge contribution: What have you done to increase the intellectual capital of the firm?
4. Reputation building: What have you done to enhance the reputation of the firm?
5. One-firm behavior: What have you done to build relationships within the firm?

It is this last category, one-firm behavior, that is critical to the functioning of matrix organizations.

Each of these general categories is further broken down into four or five specific behaviors that can be identified and observed. For example, McKinsey has its own version of one-firm behavior, which it calls "partner-like behavior." Partner-like behavior is broken down into more explicit types of behavior:

> Responsiveness: If other members of the firm ask this person for help, what is the response? How responsive is the person to the needs of the requester?

> Reaching out: Is the person proactive in identifying ways to contribute to other parts of the firm? Does the person show the initiative to mobilize an effort to contribute to another part of the firm?

> Self-interest/firm interest: When sharing revenue or costs, does the person work for a fair sharing or only pursue his or her self-interest?

Over the years, the firms try to make these subjective criteria as explicit as possible. Eventually the terms become part of the company's vocabulary.

So whether they call it one-firm behavior, partner-like behavior, or something else, the professional services firms define collaborative behaviors as key parts of people's performance. You are unlikely to become a partner if you do not score well on these criteria. You are not likely to receive a full bonus if you score poorly on this dimension. In these firms, cooperative behavior takes its place along with bringing in revenue, developing future partners, and contributing to the intellectual capital of the firm as important dimensions of performance that support the firm's strategy.

What Kind of Performance Management Process Yields a Full and Fair Assessment? One reason for being as explicit as possible about subjective criteria is that these definitions are an important step toward measuring the behaviors. Using these qualitative measures, the firms can engage in a rigorous process to apply their collective judgment. The firms are then thorough and inventive in measuring all the dimensions of a person's performance. They interview young people and use exit interviews to understand a partner's efforts at coaching and developing future partners. They interview customers and former customers to explore a partner's relationship-building performance. They engage in extensive peer reviews to assess partner-like behaviors. At General Electric, the performance assessors even gather input from the person who now has the job that the candidate last occupied. In all cases, companies attempt to collect facts or evidence of actual behavior. Sometimes these performance data are collected by using forms that are completed at the end of each assignment. McKinsey, however, prefers two-way dialogue that allows everyone on a particular client engagement to be explicit about the expected versus observed behavior.

An example of full and fair assessment is the approach employed by Latham and Watkins, a large U.S. law firm (Lorsch and Tierney, 2002, p. 70). Twice a year, the firm conducts performance reviews of all seven hundred associates. The review is conducted by a committee of partners and some senior associates. They divide the associate population into groups of twenty-five or thirty, and a committee member takes responsibility for a group. The member looks at all performance dimensions and collects performance data from all partners with whom the associates have worked; the committee member reads all the files of the associates in his or her group, analyzes comments from reviewers, follows up with conversations, and arrives at a well-documented assessment of strengths and weaknesses. The committee then meets for five or six intense days, arriving at a performance message for each associate. This performance review is used in compensation decisions, and the associates get an indication of whether they are "on track" to be considered for partner.

A similar process takes place at the partner level. At consulting firms and investment banks, a personnel committee of partners is selected to conduct a full and fair assessment process. The members of the personnel committee conduct the conversations to determine the partner's performance in all the subjective categories. Similar scrutiny applies to revenue. Although one might assume that revenue is revenue, it is not valued that way. Revenue from "house accounts" is easier to generate than revenue from new accounts, so business development revenue is more highly valued. Again subjective criteria are applied, as described earlier.

The bonus pools for these companies are based on total company revenue. At McKinsey, Bain, and others, there is one company bonus pool. Investment banks, which are larger, use all of investment banking and all of sales and trading for the bonus pool. The banks have moved away from individual department bonus pools. These departmental pools created a lot of energy and focus, but produced dysfunctional behaviors when it came to working across departments. The large pools are subjectively allocated to departments and from there to individuals. The individual bonuses are granted by the same processes described earlier. A representative from the personnel committee interviews people throughout the firm who are familiar with the person's work. At the investment banks, the interviews occur throughout the year following each large deal. The interviewer debriefs the deal team, the client, and others who are knowledgeable about the deal. The questions are "Who contributed to this deal?" and "What was the nature of their contributions?" Thus the deal revenue is not simply counted; rather, each team member's contribution is detailed by the partner doing the evaluation. All these data are then discussed by the personnel committee to get a full and fair assessment of each person's performance. The personnel committees deliberate for four or five days. Then the bonuses are announced at the end of the year.

I've described these practices to show how some high-performing matrix organizations work very hard to assess people completely and comprehensively and to reward the collaborative behaviors that are so essential to the functioning of matrix organizations. These practices are quite different than those of firms that measure only individual financial performance and only financial performance of the P&Ls. Those firms that measure only the financial performance of business units and countries encourage silo behavior. These same firms then claim that "matrix doesn't work."

Some firms mix business unit and company criteria in determining bonuses, which helps them move away from silo behavior. Other firms use subjective criteria or personal goals, the achievement of which is rewarded with a bonus. These goals are certainly valuable, but they are usually limited by the performance management process. The least effective performance management process is the one wherein the boss collects the information, makes the assessment, and decides on the bonus; this approach does not result in a full and complete assessment. In today's matrix organizations, wherein employees engage in lots of international travel, there is no way that the boss has anywhere near the necessary performance data. Besides, the boss always gets distorted information. These performance assessments are incomplete at best. It is no wonder that these firms rely on hard financial measures of performance.

The second-best performance management process is one in which the two bosses on either side of the matrix jointly evaluate the manager. This process was described in Chapter Four. At its best, the two bosses jointly agree on goals for the manager and then jointly evaluate the manager at the appropriate time. This process expands the performance categories and information that is available. Then the two bosses discuss and interpret the data to arrive at an assessment. The process takes more time than the "one-boss" assessment, but is more full and likely to be more fair.

In summary, the most full and fair process is the one described earlier. The leaders consider and measure all dimensions of performance. Then their rigorous analysis and discussion results in the assessment. There are some caveats surrounding this approach. It only works when leaders are willing to put in the time to define performance and to collect and provide performance information. It only works when people take the process seriously and give candid assessments. It only works when the leaders give bonuses in a balanced manner. At universities, performance is judged on the basis of teaching, research, and public service, but everyone knows that it is the research that counts. Professional services companies can do the same and consider only revenue. They can reward the rainmakers, and everyone will see who is really getting rewarded. So just having definitions of complete performance is not enough; the leaders of the organization must go further to deliver complete, honest, and fair assessments.

Social Capital

In addition to depending on personnel who are selected, developed, and rewarded for exhibiting collaborative behaviors, matrix organizations run on social capital. Social capital exists in organizations to the extent that there are personal networks across units and that these relationships are characterized by high trust. The best way to think of social capital is to view it as the opposite of silos: a firm that has high social capital has no silos. And doing away with solos greatly facilitates the workings of a matrix organization. Indeed, social capital is the foundation of matrix structures. So the leaders' task in implementing a matrix is to build social capital by building personal networks, valuing these networks and networkers, and developing trust along those networks.

Some of the methods of building social capital are the same ones that are used to build human capital. Social capital is often a by-product of building human capital. Recruiting and selecting networkers is one way. Rotational assignments develop multi-unit experience in managers and also develop their networks. Training sessions develop people in the skill being taught and give them exposure to twenty-five or thirty new people with whom to expand their networks. Such events as the annual meeting of the top one hundred managers is an excellent opportunity for these people to build networks among themselves. Rewarding and promoting people who behave collaboratively also has the side benefit of weakening silos. So companies are already doing a lot to build networks. Usually they can make improvements by stimulating networking at the top one hundred meeting and by selecting which twenty-five people should attend a training course together.

Leaders can also build social capital and see that it exists in the right places. The catalytic converter business that was part of the Degussa Chemical Company exemplifies how leaders can increase and focus social capital. The business's team structure was described in Chapter Eleven. It was a jewel of a business buried in a mediocre German company. It had gone from 4 percent to 20 percent worldwide market share in catalytic converters. The leaders of this business saw their competitive advantage as being their process for new product development. This process was consistently delivering customized, high-quality products that the customer wanted and on a very short development cycle.

The unique feature of this business's leadership was that they saw their competitive advantage as rooted in their organization. Ahead of competitors, they created customer teams that rapidly developed customer-specific products. The leaders managed a matrix structure of customer teams across functions. They saw the critical link in the new product development process to be the transition of the product from the R&D labs to the factory. The R&D-manufacturing interface needed to be seamless. Historically, however, it was a bottleneck. So when the new leadership team was formed, it led a redesign of the new product development process. The new process was designed around simultaneous engineering. That is, the manufacturing engineers were brought into the new product development effort early in the process. As a matter of fact, they were colocated with the product design engineers. Manufacturing engineering liaison offices were established in the R&D labs; R&D offices were likewise placed at factories where new products were launched. Engineers from the factories rotated through these liaison offices, and R&D people rotated through the factories. On each new launch (one launch for every new customer engine), several R&D engineers stayed with the product and moved into manufacturing. So through colocation and rotations, the leaders were trying to build personal networks between R&D and the factory, destroying the silos.

A cross-functional team was appointed to debrief the experience following each new product introduction. These were people who were not part of that product team. They would assess the launch, identify the lessons learned, and offer ideas for process improvement. The purpose of the team was to produce an assessment of the launch, but there were also the by-products of teaching people from the functions about the new product development process and building cross-functional networks. These assessments went to the head of R&D, who was the process owner.

Once a year, the heads of R&D and manufacturing reviewed these assessments with each factory and laboratory pair. The managements of both attended a two-day off-site to review the past year's results. They celebrated the improvements and identified and fixed the problems. The two heads of R&D and manufacturing always attended together and modeled the cooperation they wanted to see. They always had an overnight meeting so that informal conversations and a nice dinner could be used to build personal networks across the labs and plants. These assessments and reviews became an important part of the reward system in the two functions. When difficult individuals would obstruct the launch, they were moved to other positions. High performers at the interface would become candidates for rotations and promotions.

In this way, the leadership continuously managed the workings at the interface. They constantly improved the process. At the same time, they continuously invested their own time and effort in building social capital. They built the relationships and the trust necessary to launch new products. They actually saw their organization as their competitive advantage and invested to keep it an advantage.

The building of social capital is the final important organization design feature that is built (or not built) through many of the HR policies. Aside from following the HR policies, the leadership must value social capital and work to create it themselves. If they do not, they can expect silos to result.

Summary

This chapter described the HR policies that fit with a matrix organization. Leaders start by identifying the kind of people who will thrive in their matrix. They then engage in recruiting, selecting, training, and developing people who show the right behaviors. These same behaviors are measured and rewarded through a full and fair performance assessment process. These HR processes, such as recruiting and the creating of subjective assessments, require leaders to establish shared values and to expend the time and effort necessary to support the candid assessments. These practices related to the development of human capital round out the aligned Star Model for a completely designed matrix organization. When put into effect by a leadership group that values its organization, these HR policies will eliminate silos and build the social capital underlying the matrix behaviors. Success requires investments in both human and social capital.

13

LEADERSHIP IN A MATRIX ORGANIZATION

A key component in the design of matrix organizations is a strong leader at the top of the matrix. The top of a matrix exists anywhere that the two or three sides of a matrix come together. It is at these points that the natural tensions and conflicts of a matrix come together and need to be resolved. When these natural conflicts are resolved effectively and expediently, the matrix works well. When they are not resolved, the matrix flounders. So the leadership role is a critical one. It is also a frequently occurring role throughout the organization. These roles must be staffed with people who can encourage the escalation of issues, hear people out, and make a decision if the people involved cannot achieve consensus.

The leadership role in a matrix organization has several dimensions in addition to its conflict resolution aspect. As I've discussed elsewhere, the top team needs to engage in lively debate before conflicts can be resolved; the leader must be a capable leader of the top team to ensure that effective debate takes place. The leader also needs to be a good power balancer (Davis and Lawrence, 1977), which entails, first, possessing a deep and nuanced understanding of the power levers in the organization and, second, being skilled in the use of these levers to shape the decisions being made in the teams throughout the matrix. These leaders need to see that the distribution of power inside their matrix is aligned with the power requirements in their business environment. For example, if the power of the customer is increasing, the leaders must ensure that the internal customer champion, usually sales, is likewise empowered. Let's look now at each of these leadership roles.

Seeing That Conflicts Are Resolved

The leader does not have to have the final word on all conflicts. However, he or she must see that all conflicts are effectively resolved. It is the tough calls that will come to the leader's team, and some may require the leader to be a tiebreaker in a timely manner. The leader's tasks are to create and manage the context for resolving these conflicts, manage the leadership team's process, and make the tough call when needed.

To create the context for resolving conflicts, leaders must first establish values and norms such that people in the organization understand that conflict is normal and natural, not a sign of a dysfunctional company. Second, leaders must design and maintain the connected set of teams and relationships shown in Figure 10.2. Third, leaders need to provide the team participants with the training and infrastructure to support their decision making. Finally, the top team itself needs to be a model of how the consensus-driven conflict resolution process works.

Create the Acceptance of Conflict as Normal and Natural

The main message to be communicated by the leader is that conflict is a natural consequence of being in a matrix structure. Too often people react with alarm to the increase in conflict that results from introducing a matrix. They think that conflict is a sign that the organizational change isn't working and that there is now organizational discord. Nothing could be further from the truth. When conflict arises, it indicates that the structure is working. It should surface differences between the two or three sides of the matrix. As a matter of fact, the absence of conflict should indicate that the matrix is not working. Absence means that the natural conflicts are being hidden and acted out in dysfunctional ways.

The surfacing and resolving of conflicts is identical to the surfacing and fixing of problems in the Toyota Production System (TPS) or lean manufacturing process. The TPS has eliminated inventories and created a flow process. The TPS is therefore specifically designed to be sensitive to supply or quality problems, which are then surfaced and solved immediately on the spot. The norms and values of Toyota emphasize that discovering a problem is discovering a jewel. Doing so allows you to fix a problem that you did not know you had. People who find problems are praised. They come to work every day looking for problems in order to continuously improve the process. Prior to the implementation of lean manufacturing, people in organizations would hide problems. People who surfaced problems were blamed for them. It was best to cover up issues and to avoid the scrutiny of a punitive supervisor.

The same situation exists with a matrix organization. The addition of a second and third dimension to the structure adds people who see the world differently. Matrix structures are *designed* to generate conflict. The country manager wants a local solution to a situation. The addition of a business unit manager brings the addition of a global solution to the same situation. A conflict of opinions results. The matrix is based on the assumption that the two managers will problem-solve and find a third solution that is both global and local. It assumes that the product managers and functional managers will problem-solve and create a third solution that yields functional excellence and fast time to market. Effective resolution will only happen, however, if the people approach the conflicts with the appropriate mind-sets and skill sets.

The leader's task is to see that people approach these conflicts with the mind-set that conflict is natural and that it should be resolved through problem solving; he or she must also ensure that people in the matrix have the problem-solving skills to resolve the conflict. Not everyone responds to a conflict with problem-solving behavior. Some may try to win the situation; the best way to win is often by not sharing all information or distorting the situation. Others will compromise, or "split the difference." Still others will smooth over the differences and act as if there is no conflict. These responses do not lead to the creation of new options to resolve the issue. In general, they are less effective. Leaders communicate the appropriate mind-set through their normal message sending and their own behavior. They reinforce it by rewarding and managing it through the performance management process.

Design and Maintain the Connected Set of Teams

The second task of the leader in managing conflicts is to design the team structure described in Chapter Ten and maintain its conflict-generating and conflict-resolving apparatus. Recall that in a business-region matrix, as shown in Figure 13.1, there is

Figure 13.1: Interconnected Teams in a Business-Region Matrix

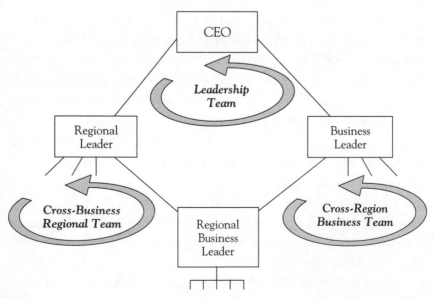

a cross-regional business team run by the business leaders, and a cross-business regional team run by the regional leader. Each team prepares a strategy, plan, and budget for the upcoming time period. The goals are displayed in a spreadsheet in which the businesses are the rows and the regions are the columns. The planning process is the means by which conflict is both generated and resolved. The teams first try to problem-solve in order to align the goals of regions and businesses. The key role here is that of the regional business leader, who is a member of both teams. This individual uses his or her pivotal role to arrive at a plan and budget that meets the strategies of both the region and the business. When the teams are unable to get to an agreement, their two leaders try to find a solution. Failing that, the issue goes to a debate at the level of the leadership team. This system of connected teams is intended to align most of the goals at the team level. New and difficult issues then make their way up the chain to the leadership team. One hopes that precedent-setting policy issues are the ones that arise.

The subject of escalation can be controversial. I hold the position that the escalation process is a critical one. The leader or the company needs to establish an explicit escalation process for the matrix. Everyone agrees that the best resolution to a conflict is one reached on the spot by the parties themselves. But what happens when they cannot resolve it? If the impasse is a result of the two parties being simply unable to agree, that is unhealthy, but they may need help. If the impasse occurs because the two parties do not have all the information they need or because it's a new issue, then escalation is necessary. I would encourage escalation in both cases. One reason is to get a decision, a timely decision. But more important, every escalation is a coaching opportunity. In the first case, the parties may need help coming to an agreement, or perhaps they require a reprimand. Some pointers from the boss or a facilitator may be needed. In the second and other cases, the leader needs to provide an explanation in addition to a decision. In all cases, therefore, the leader does not simply make a decision. He or she should make a decision but also provide both coaching and some interpretation or communication so that the parties will understand the rationale behind the decision. The parties may use this logic in the event that a similar issue comes up.

The leader should encourage escalation, especially in a new matrix. The issues will inform the leader and serve as opportunities for coaching. The leader should also encourage joint escalation of issues. If the leader hears two individual and partial views of the same situation, a decision is hard to come by. The skilled leader calls both parties in together and insists on a complete explanation. The leader should make joint escalation a company-wide process.

The leader is responsible for the workings of these teams. Often the planning process owner is the one delegated the task of operating the connected system of teams, as described in Chapter Ten. But the leader needs to see that a complete Star Model is created and maintained for this connected team planning process. The leader does this, in part, by ensuring that the goals from planning feed into the performance management system, and the teams are staffed with the type of people who will make them work. These team members establish goals through the planning process and are peer assessed in the performance management process as well. The leader should also hold a review with the process owner to see that the process is working satisfactorily. In addition, the leader can make informal assessments through discussions with the participants.

There are two useful diagnostics for assessing how the connected team process is being implemented. One is for the leader to directly assess the escalation process. He or she can ask such questions as "Are we getting the escalations that are appropriate?" "Are there too many or too few?" "Are disagreements moving too quickly or too slowly through the process?" The leader and the process owner can then make improvements. The second indicator is the team members' satisfaction. These are also the people with two bosses. When conflicts are not being resolved or dysfunctional behaviors are occurring, these people are aware of them and are often impacted by them. So some intelligence gathering involving them is a good practice to implement. Focus groups of these people, interviews by the process owner, or e-mail surveys are all good ways to collect this intelligence. Again, the leader and the process owner or the leadership team can develop some improvements. The important point is to continuously monitor the workings of the matrix and the teams and provide quick corrective action.

Provide the Training and Infrastructure to Support the Matrix

This decision shaper is fairly straightforward. The participants in the matrix need the skill sets to manage the conflicts and the group problem solving that are intrinsic to the workings of a matrix. Indeed, the inability to manage conflict in a healthy manner has been the cause of a number of failures of matrix implementations. Even today, conflict remains a major challenge. Mastering it requires some investment in skill development.

There are any number of group problem-solving and conflict management processes, but by far the best practice is to establish a company-wide process. At Intel, for example, all new employees are trained in Intel's conflict resolution process. Then when conflicts arise, the employees can remain focused on the issues themselves and not be distracted by the means of addressing them. The process is posted on the wall in all conference rooms, providing a shared language that everyone can use so as to achieve resolution more quickly. IBM too has a common process for conflict management. It also offers online resources to which parties to a conflict can refer. An intranet tool walks the parties through some questions and suggestions for handling an impasse. There are suggestions regarding when to escalate and when to work out differences at their own level. If the suggestions do not work, the parties can ask facilitators to assist.

In summary, the provision of training and skill development helps greatly in the conflict resolution process. Some backup infrastructure like that at IBM can help as well. These actions, together with creating the decision-shaping designs and the appropriate context, round out one of the leader's roles. The second leadership role is that of managing the top team in a way that models best practice.

Managing the Top Team

I have referred several times to the importance of the leader's ability to manage the top team. The important point is that the leadership group at the top of a matrix needs to be managed as a team. The matrix structure makes all the managers reporting to the leader interdependent, which means that issues affect some or all managers simultaneously; conflict is often inherent to the situation. These issues must be dealt with collectively. The leader needs to follow a process to hear all sides and get a total picture, to lead a discussion of the issue, and finally to arrive at a timely decision.

There are a variety of ways to manage this interdependence appropriately. The way *not* to manage it is with a one-on-one or hub-and-spoke management style. Often this style results when a boss is not strong enough to publicly mediate disputes between strong subordinates. This style is often characterized by the expression, "The one who wins a dispute around here is the one who left the boss's office last," meaning that the boss hears only partial and biased views on an individual basis from the parties to an interdependent situation, is swayed by the views of others, and allows the last view that he or she heard to determine the outcome. I wish that this situation were rare in today's management environment, but it is not. I have a client who is guilty of this kind of behavior. The top team goes through a debate and arrives at an allocation of the R&D budget across businesses and across regions. One of the regional presidents is often disappointed. So the next time the CEO visits the region, the president and the CEO go to dinner, and after a few glasses of wine the president rolls out the R&D budget. Often the president gets a little more funding through this backdoor channel. Nothing destroys teamwork and trust faster than these kinds of deals. Remember, matrix runs on social capital, personal networks, and reasonable levels of trust.

The preferred way of dealing with top team issues is to get the right collection of people around the table. The appropriate number could be two, three, or five, but in any case the leader brings all the parties to an issue in on the discussion. Then the group gets the data out, defines the issue, and creates some options. It is critical to come up with more than two options. There is always a local option from the country manager and a global option from the business unit head. The discussion can easily polarize around these two options. Each side tries to convince the other, resulting in a dialogue of the deaf. Good leaders get at least one more option to break the log jam. Remember that the benefit of the global matrix is the creation of solutions that may be 70 percent global and 30 percent local one time and 60 percent local and 40 percent global the next time. The options may or may not need to be analyzed and evaluated outside the meeting. If there is a need for further data gathering and analysis, then quickly convene a follow-up meeting to make a final decision. The group may reach a consensus, or the leader may decide. But this kind of process gets all the views out and surfaces third and fourth options.

A current client has evolved a way of managing conflicts in the global matrix. The CEO does not like to run meetings. I was told, "He's not a meeting guy." So disputes are jointly escalated to the COO and CEO by the parties. The COO prepares agendas and runs the meetings. Almost all disputes get resolved between these four people—the CEO, the COO, the regional manager, and the business manager. Larger meetings are run by the CEO's direct reports. HR runs the talent reviews and the bonus allocations, the CFO runs the financial reviews, and so on. The CEO is present and will decide on issues when required. Usually he wants to think about many of the issues and, after "sleeping on it," will decide in one or two days. Worth noting is that he will not be swayed by and actually discourages individual lobbying in the interim. The best way to influence the boss in this organization is to make and defend your argument in front of your peers.

In summary, the strong matrix leader

- Encourages and only accepts joint escalations
- Gets the right people around the table or on speaker phones
- Listens to all the data from all the parties
- Encourages multiple options beyond the two preferred ones
- Works for a consensus among the parties
- Makes a decision when there is no consensus
- Discourages backdoor lobbying
- Informs all parties of the decision so as to maintain joint accountability
- Explains the business logic behind the decision so that the next time managers can resolve the issue themselves

Following this process takes a lot of discipline, but results in a better-functioning matrix. Doing so also sends powerful signals throughout the company about how to behave in a matrix.

Balancing Power

The third role of the matrix leader is the balancing and aligning of power across the matrix and with the external business environment. This role is like that of any leader; in a matrix, however, organization power and authority exist in a more delicate balance. The company typically is simultaneously organized around the three dimensions of functions, businesses, and geographies. In this matrix, the power and authority distributed to these three dimensions are quite closely balanced, but the balance can be disturbed by external events, crises, and normal power struggles. The leader's task is to maintain or change this balance to keep it aligned with the strategy.

One of the strengths of the matrix organization is its flexibility in distributing power. If a shift in power to the business side is required, the leader can assign a stronger leader or increase the business budget. In a geographically organized company, a disruptive reorganization to business units would be required. In the hands of a sophisticated leader, a matrix can dial up the power on the business side and dial down the geographic side, or vice versa. A matrix should allow this flexibility in altering the distribution of power and therefore the type of decision outcomes that are produced. Let's look at how leaders balance power and how they align it with external events.

Managing Power Distributions

The leader can manage the real-time distribution of power and authority by using any and all of the power levers described in Chapter Five. The leader can have any activity report to her directly for any period of time. She can appoint a talented person to the role, give him a budget, physically locate him on the top floor, assign specific decision authority to him, and so on. In most matrix structures, this balancing is a continuous task for the leader.

If the leader follows my advice and manages the top team as a team, more real-time opportunities to balance power present themselves. The top team then engages in problem solving and decision making in the group. The decisions are actually made right in front of the leader. As decisions are made, the leader can throw his weight behind a proposal from an underpowered participant, define criteria from the strategy, protect a minority viewpoint, and so on. In this way, the leader can align the decision-making power with the needs of the business in real time.

Aligning Power with the Business Environment

In a world where the balance of power is continuously shifting among customers, institutions, suppliers, and governments, the leader needs to ensure that power is shifting inside the company to reflect the external reality. However, within organizations this shift of power usually does not happen automatically. The leader has to make it happen. And it happens by using the same power levers I've already mentioned. But this time the leader is guided by a stakeholder analysis and a monitoring of shifts in influence among those stakeholders.

In Chapter One and again in Chapter Nine, we followed the shift in power at multinationals away from country managers. The process of global integration shifted decision-making power to people with cross-border responsibilities, such as functional and business unit heads. In the 1990s, the global customer began insisting on being serviced as a global customer. The result was a shift in power to global account managers inside the vendors to these customers. So far this century, western firms are targeting growth in Brazil, Russia, India, and China, the so-called BRIC group. And because each of these economies is regulated, has a host government that is active in the economic process, and has state-owned enterprises, we are seeing the return of the country manager. Each of these changes had to be led by the person at the top of the matrix; otherwise the status quo would have prevailed.

These power shifts also require a strong leader. Often the leader is alone or in the minority in seeing a need for change. Ironically, the organization's leader must be an antiestablishment figure. Strength is required to convince others or move them to other positions. But when successful, these shifts demonstrate the strength of the matrix structure.

Summary

This chapter has made the case for a strong leader at the top of the matrix. First, the top is where disputes come for resolution. The leader needs to be comfortable in leading the conflict resolution processes and making decisions when needed. The leader needs to manage this whole decision-making process. Second, the leader needs to create a top team that behaves as a team. These people are usually strong personalities themselves. The proper method is to avoid one-on-one deals and backdoor lobbying. The leader needs to keep the issues in front of people and get the whole story before deciding. Third, the leader is the power balancer. It is best to have a leader who is sophisticated at using the power levers in the organization. But very often, the leaders need to use themselves to tilt the power situation. The status quo usually needs someone in a leadership position to tip the balance of power.

This same type of strength will be needed by leaders who lead the changes to implement a matrix. Change management and culture building are the topics of the next chapter.

14

IMPLEMENTING A MATRIX

One of the reasons for the failure of many of the early attempts to implement a matrix was the change management process. As I noted in the Introduction, many change processes were nonexistent, inappropriate, or incomplete. Today it is a rare company that attempts a strategic change without a well-planned, well-managed change process. There are plenty of books written on managing change (see Beer and Nohria, 2000). And by now, it should be clear that I recommend a complete change by aligning all the elements of the Star Model with the strategy and with each other. But there is still the question of where to start on the Star Model. And does the sequence make a difference? And if some of the early attempts were inappropriate, what constitutes an appropriate change process? Let me address those issues in this chapter on implementing a matrix.

Using the Star Model

Questions that I hear frequently are "Where do you start on the Star Model?" and "Is there a preferred sequence for moving around it?" My answer is, "You can start anywhere." If a company is having trouble with its compensation system, I start there. The first question then is, "What kind of compensation system do we need?" The answer is, "It depends on the strategy." Thus all roads lead to strategy. I start where the pain is or where the clients' energy is. That starting point will lead to strategy, structure, and process eventually.

I do have a preferred starting point and sequence. I prefer to start with strategy. If the strategy is not sufficiently clear, then I will not change structure until it is. Some additional strategy work may be needed. Once the strategy is clear enough (it does not have to be 100 percent complete before you can start on structure), the structure changes can be created. The strategy is clear enough when you can formulate the design criteria for evaluating structural options. So I move from strategy to structure to processes. What processes do we need to coordinate across the structure? From the processes, we can determine the performance measures and behaviors. Then we can design the performance management and reward systems. Finally we can create the recruiting profiles and employee value propositions. In this way, I prefer to work clockwise around the Star Model. Many organization design consulting engagements come close to following the preferred modus operandi. (See Galbraith, 2002, chap. 10 for more details.)

An example is a client that implemented a global line-of-business matrix across its existing region and country structure. The new CEO felt that there was a need for more coordination within a line of business and across countries. He created a number of global forums, essentially cross-border teams for common business lines. Their task was to prepare some thinking and concepts as to whether it was a good idea to form global lines of business. "What would be the positives and what would be the negatives?" Six months later, he scheduled the first annual global conference for the top 150 people, at which the global forums reported their findings. I was invited to speak to the conference about global matrix organizations. The feedback from the conference was positive, and I was invited to work with the leadership to develop some next steps.

At the end of six more months, the company announced an organizational change to a matrix using the two-hat model. That is, the regional managers in the existing structure were given responsibility for a global line of business in addition to their region. They were to build on the work done by the global forums and use the teams to further develop the global strategies.

They were to prepare a plan and budget that would form a spreadsheet of businesses across regions. In nine months, they held a budget conference of all the teams and put together a budget that was presented to the board and that served as their financial plan for the next fiscal year.

Thus this company started with some strategic ideas that were produced by the global forums. These ideas led to a structure change at the top to a two-hat model matrix. This new structure implemented the spreadsheet planning and budgeting process. It was a change in strategy that led to a change in structure and then process. At this point the change was still flexible. If the strategy formulation led to a conclusion that the new global business strategies did not make sense, the business lines could be dropped and the geographic structure could be continued as before. It was still a time for testing out global ideas. As it turned out, the results indicated that further steps were in order.

The CEO made a couple of personnel changes at this point. Two of the regional managers had a great deal of difficulty with the idea of moving to stronger business lines and had problems with working in a matrix organization. One of them took early retirement, and the other went on a special assignment with the intention of retiring in a couple of years. The fact that two of the leaders could not make the change is not at all unusual. When personnel changes are required, the CEO must step up and make them. They send strong signals to the rest of the organization that the change is now a permanent one. The company is moving to a matrix organization.

The company went outside to recruit two new regional managers. Both of them came from companies using global matrix organizations. The structure was changed such that the regions and the lines of business now reported to the CEO. The eight lines of business reported through a single person who functioned like a COO lite. A new HR leader was brought in; this individual is now leading a redesign of the performance management system and the implementation of a more judgmental bonus process that will reward cooperative behaviors. Also being redesigned are the hiring profiles and recruitment process. Thus, over two years, the entire Star Model has been redesigned for the two top levels of the structure. The process is continuing with a development program for the top 150. The program content going forward covers how a matrix works, teamwork skills, and conflict management processes and skills. The CEO or the heads of the various lines of business comes on the last day to hear from the group how the matrix is working and what their suggestions are for improvements.

Building Capabilities

Another approach to change is to build the capabilities that underlie the matrix first, then change the structure. Let us take the example of financial services (FS) firms and the globalization of their customers. Most FS firms were traditionally organized by country and by service or product lines, as described earlier. Figure 14.1 shows an investment bank with countries as primary profit centers. Within each country, relationship managers served customers and called on specialists in the service or product lines when the customers needed their services. The product lines, such as foreign exchange (Fx) and mergers and acquisitions, were the secondary profit centers. By the late 1980s, however, global customers wanted cash management and Fx to be provided in every country where they were present. These customers began to select FS firms for their ability to provide integrated service. Many of the large multinational FS firms saw that they needed to change their organizations and build a capability to coordinate across countries. To do this, the FS firms employed formal structures: such integrating mechanisms as teams and coordinators. They mobilized these mechanisms in a sequence of steps. The next sections look at a six-step sequence as an example.

Figure 14.1: Structure of Investment Bank (c. 1990)

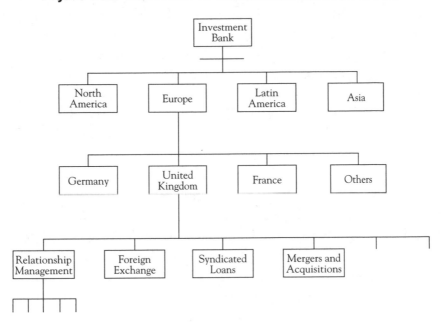

A Few Customer Teams

An initial step taken by many FS firms was to create approximately five customer teams to serve customers around the world. The firms carefully chose the five customers who were most desirous of this global service. The account manager serving the customer's headquarters was the team leader. A team member was also selected in each country where the customer wanted service. This team then put together and executed an integrated customer strategy and plan.

Two things usually result from this effort. One is the intended outcome: better coordination across countries to deliver integrated service to the global customer. The other is the opening up of new opportunities: first, the opportunity to drive organizational change and, second, the opportunity to build organizational capability.

The first opportunity is provided by satisfied customers. They can become a genuine force for change. If they have been carefully selected, these customers should respond positively to improved service across countries; but they will also indicate that more effort is needed to meet their needs. This outside force, an increasingly satisfied customer that still wants more, can be used to change country-focused mind-sets.

Then there is the opportunity to expand and build on the capability already created. With each customer team consisting of 50 to 60 people, between 250 and 300 people have now become aware of and part of the change effort. There are now 300 people who are trained in cross-border customer strategies, who understand the needs of the global customer, and who have cross-border networks and personal contacts. The 300 people too can become a positive force for change. They will have had different experiences. Most experiences should be positive, if people were chosen and recruited on the basis of their skills and interests. Some of these people will enjoy the experience and want more. Some will find that serving local clients is more to their liking and can opt out. If management is observant, the customer teams serve as an audition to find cross-border talent. Some people will be good at this new effort and others not. Managements that see their task as identifying new leadership can use the teams as an opportunity to do so. And finally, the effort provides a learning experience. By collecting team members' and customers' experiences and ideas, management can improve the customer team structure when future teams are created for other customers.

These two outcomes are produced at each step in the change sequence. To summarize, the first outcome is the improved execution of some task. This outcome remains the intended purpose of the change. But the second outcome is the opportunity for management to engage outsiders, such as customers; change the mind-sets of the doubters; train agents of change; build personal networks; select and develop new leaders; and improve the process. Managements that capture these opportunities can use changes to cross-country teams to drive and shape organizational change and begin the transition to a matrix organization.

More Customer Teams

A next step would be to expand from a handful to a dozen or so customer teams. Again the firm selects those customers that want integrated service. The firm can solicit volunteers or carefully select team members who are interested in cross-border work. The previous team members can also solicit their colleagues to join. Usually the firm can make these team assignments attractive. In FS firms, people are interested in personal growth and opportunity. Working on a team serving a global customer can be a route to learning and development not available with local clients. The multinational customer is usually the most advanced customer. Management can also ensure that work on global customer teams is recognized and rewarded in the countries.

Outcomes from this effort should resemble those from the first step. The difference is the larger number of people involved. Instead of a few hundred, this time a thousand or more people are trained in serving global customers and building their networks. A couple of dozen satisfied customers are asking for more. A critical mass of change agents is being built.

Global Accounts Coordinator

The next step is to create a position on the management team to coordinate the efforts to serve the global customer. At a minimum, this change gives the global customer a voice or a champion on the management team. Someone of higher status can now appeal to recalcitrant country managers. The global accounts coordinator will expand the number of teams again. But perhaps most important, the coordinator can fund and build a customer-focused infrastructure. This change creates a geography-dominant matrix with a customer lite axis.

One task is to create a common process for building global customer plans and strategies. Initially, some experimenting by customer teams is useful. But the countries soon get overwhelmed with fifteen different planning formats. The coordinator can collect best practices from the various teams and set up a task force staffed with veterans of global teams to create common guidelines, forms, and processes. The common process makes it easier for customer teams and country management to work together.

The next task is the design and building of customer-based information and accounting systems. The question always arises, "Are we making any money serving these global customers?" With country-based accounting systems and profit centers, it is usually impossible to tell. Depending on whether the countries have compatible systems or not, this change can be a major effort requiring central funding and leadership from the global accounts coordinator. But in the end, the customer teams will have information with which to measure their progress, compare their performance with other teams, and demonstrate global profitability.

A way to combine these two tasks is to generate revenue and profit targets for customers in the planning process. The teams can have revenue and profit goals for their global customers in each country. Perhaps more important, the goals can be added up in each country. Then each country manager can have revenue and profit goals for local clients and global accounts and can get credit for and be held accountable for these targets. The accounting system must connect the costs and revenues associated with each global customer. For example, an account team in the London office of one of the large investment banks worked for a year to win the global business of a big U.K. firm. The team succeeded in winning the contract, but most of the work for the next few years would be in the North American subsidiary and in a recent acquisition in Australia. That meant that the work plus the costs to win the business were incurred in the United Kingdom, but the revenues would be booked in North America and Australia. With customer profit accounting, the U.K. office can identify the revenues and costs and receive credit. The targets can be adjusted for these disconnects. Thus, in addition to being a champion for the customer, the global accounts coordinator can create the processes and information systems to manage the global customer as well as continue to develop and identify talent and leadership on the teams.

Global Accounts Group

As the number of global accounts and teams exceeds several hundred, the role of the global accounts coordinator can be expanded and taken on by a department or a group. Customers and teams are grouped into broadly defined industry categories, such as consumer products, financial services, oil and gas, pharmaceuticals and life sciences, multimedia, and so on. Although these groupings facilitate supervision of accounts, their main purpose is to satisfy customers. Customers want bankers who understand their business. Pharmaceutical companies assume that their bankers understand the NDA process and know what the Human Genome Project is all about. So the global accounts activity can be expanded and specialized by customer segment.

The global accounts group usually leads an effort to establish a common segmentation scheme across the company. In large countries like Germany, the United Kingdom, and Japan, customer segments are probably already in use. What is important is to have compatible schemes across the countries. Then a one-to-one interface can be established to facilitate communication between countries and within industries. The global accounts group usually includes global industry coordination: a global industry coordinator is selected for each industry that is common across the countries.

Many companies experience the need for global coordinating but have few people who are qualified to fill the roles. But if a company has followed the steps presented in this book and used the opportunity created by the initial customer team implementations described in this chapter, the company should have grown its own talent by the time it has reached this stage.

An audit firm can again serve as the example. A young Swiss auditor was identified as a talented performer on audits of banks in Zurich. When a global team was created for Citibank, the auditor, who had experience in audits of Citibank's subsidiary, became the Swiss representative on the Citibank team. On the basis of his good performance, the auditor agreed to an assignment in the United Kingdom. The move gave the auditor the opportunity to work in the London financial center. While in London, the auditor served as the U.K. representative on the Credit Suisse global team. His next assignment was to lead an in-depth audit of the Credit Suisse First Boston investment bank in the United States. The auditor was then made partner of the audit firm and returned to Zurich. From there he was selected to be the global accounts team leader for Credit Suisse. After several years in the team leader role, the auditor became the global coordinator for the financial services customer segment. The firm assessed the auditor in each assignment for audit performance and knowledge of the financial services industry as usual. But it also assessed his teamwork skills, relationships with customers, ability to influence without authority, cross-cultural skills with customers and team members, and leadership of the cross-border team. Through his experiences and training courses, the auditor was qualified to move into the global coordinator role.

Global Accounts and Countries Matrix

A next step, designed to shift more power to the teams serving global customers, is to carve out global accounts units within countries and dedicate them to the global customers. The other country units will serve local customers. The global units report to the global accounts coordinator and to the local country manager in a matrix structure. These country units place dedicated talent in the service of the global customer. This change is a move to the balanced matrix form.

In some small countries, the country management may be reluctant to create a dedicated unit and share in its direction. They may have a surplus of profitable local business and prefer to avoid the multinationals. In these cases, several FS firms have created joint ventures between the headquarters and the local country management. Usually the dedicated unit is funded from headquarters and staffed initially with expatriates. After a couple of years, the local managers usually notice that the unit is quite profitable. In addition, they notice that the unit is a positive factor in recruiting; many new hires are attracted by the opportunity to work with global firms. In this way, the creation of a global customer joint venture changes local mind-sets. Local management eventually takes over the staffing and shares in the administration of the global unit.

Some firms stop here and operate as a balanced customer-country matrix. Others take another step.

Customer Profit Centers

A final step is to establish customers and customer segments as the line organization and profit centers. All the global units report to the global industry units. The countries manage the local business and serve as geographic coordinators. This change is the move to create a customer-dominant matrix structure.

Citibank followed a similar stepwise process with its commercial banking business. Starting in 1985, the bank reestablished its World Corporations Group (WCG), which managed global corporations across its country profit center structure. The group created a team for each global account. Team members were subsidiary account managers, and the team leader was a global account manager. The number of Citibank customers qualifying to become global accounts increased to around 450. The WCG created a customer-focused planning system and an accounting system to track customer revenue, cost, and profit across countries.

In 1995, Citibank conducted a strategy study. The leaders came to appreciate the fact that it was a bank (took deposits and made loans in local currencies) in more than one hundred countries. The nearest competitor was Hongkong and Shanghai Banking Company (now HSBC), with presence in around forty-three countries. Citibank's global presence was a competitive advantage that could not be matched by competitors. It chose to become a cross-border bank. It would focus on global products, such as foreign exchange and cash management, for global customers. Each of thirteen hundred global customers became a profit center. The bank collected these customers into global industry groupings for administration. The customer-focused planning process is now called COMPASS and is placed on an intranet. Thus, in about twelve years, Citibank shifted from country profit centers to customer profit centers. It used a balanced matrix structure as an evolutionary step along the way. It evolved its strategy, structure, and systems. It drove the change with formal integrating mechanisms, such as customer teams and global account coordinators, before completing it with the establishment of a new formal structure, a customer-dominant matrix.

In general, management can drive a change process to transform any existing organization into any new organization using the sequential approach. Each step in the sequence makes an incremental shift in the power structure, as shown in Figure 14.2.

Each increment corresponds to the change in one of the six steps outlined in the previous sections. The downward sloping line partitions the power distribution between the old structure and the new. At Citibank, the old structure was country dominant and the new one is customer dominant. Notice that the matrix is a power balance. Starting with a few teams and moving to stronger coordinating units, the steps effect the gradual transfer of power from countries (existing structure) to customers (new structure). At each step, new work is accomplished. In the FS firms, the new work was cross-country coordination

Figure 14.2: Shifting Power Incrementally to a New Structure

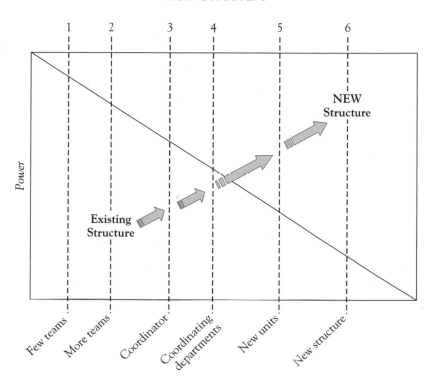

to provide integrated service to the global customer. At each step there is also the opportunity to drive and shape the change process. With teams (steps 1 and 2), a few hundred and then a thousand people learn about the global customer. They learn how to create strategies that competitors cannot match. A percentage of the participants will become advocates for change and will lobby the nonbelievers. Through the teams, a thousand people will build networks of personal contacts.

Management's role is to seize the opportunity and drive the change. Leaders may sponsor a formal development program, such as training sessions for team members. These sessions can facilitate more learning and networking; also, management and customers can attend and get feedback from the participants.

But most important is the opportunity for management to select and develop the talent and leadership for the new strategy and structure. By observing and reviewing the teams, management can identify people with the skills for and interest in cross-border work in a matrix organization. Who are the best potential team members? Who can be a team leader? Who can develop into a global industry coordinator? Who can influence without authority?

The coordinator roles (steps 3, 4, and 5) shift more power to the new structure and deliver more service to the customer. But the other opportunity is to develop processes and information systems to support the new organization. In addition, the coordinator teaches management about the new strategy. The company must shift from managing a portfolio of countries to managing a portfolio of customers as well. How will it make trade-offs and set priorities? At each step, management has the opportunity to change the soft factors to support the change. Leaders can develop the talent, build the networks, change the mind-sets, and ultimately create a cross-border customer-focused culture.

In this example, the firms started with a few customers and built the matrix capabilities as they expanded the number of customer teams. In the end they built a global customer-country matrix. In the first example (at the beginning of the chapter) the company changed the whole company to a business-region matrix. However, it changed only the top two layers. It is evolving by cascading from the top to the rest of the organization. In each case, the firm tackles a change to part of the organization and builds a whole Star Model. Then it moves to another part of the structure until it is complete. This model is an appropriate change model. Many of the early implementations of matrix attempted to change the entire organization at once. These companies did not build capabilities. They encountered considerable resistance along the way. A new leader would then be appointed, who would terminate the change effort. On the front page of the

Wall Street Journal, the new leader would say, "We tried matrix management, and it didn't work. We have buried the matrix." Today we keep the amount of change undertaken within the bounds of the company's ability to absorb it. The company builds matrix capabilities as it grows and changes and thereby extends the bounds of its ability to implement a matrix.

The other lesson from the example is that matrix can be used as a permanent form of organization or can be a temporary stepping-stone along the way when evolving from one structure to another. Citibank used it to evolve from using country profit centers to using customer profit centers. Intel used matrix to evolve from a single business strategy and thus functional organization to a multi–profit center, multibusiness divisional organization. In all cases, the companies build capabilities along the way in the transition. So matrix can be useful when power shifting as well as power balancing.

Summary

This chapter addressed the process of implementing a matrix. The primary message of the chapter, and indeed the whole book, is to create a complete and aligned Star Model. A second message is to use a collaborative means of implementation, as described in chap. 10 of *Designing Organizations* (Galbraith, 2002). Matrix is an inherently collaborative structure. Therefore you use a collaborative means to introduce it and practice the skills that will be needed to run it. A third message is to keep the amount of change within the bounds of the company's ability to absorb it. Trying to install a matrix in the whole company before building the capabilities is a surefire way to inoculate it against ever trying to install a matrix in the future. To avoid this fate, we examined two alternative approaches. In the first, the company changed structure first, but only the top two levels. Then managers in the new roles developed the processes, rewards, and people practices. The change was then cascaded to the next levels, and the top 150 were trained in matrix skills. At each step, the change involved a complete Star Model.

The other example was that of the financial services firms and Citibank in particular. They developed the capabilities and people over time. As a matter of fact, the last thing that Citibank did was change the structure. It used the time before the structure change to develop the accounting systems, the share-of-wallet planning systems, the customer teams, training, and so on.

In Chapter Fifteen, we look at the capabilities needed to implement a successful matrix organization.

15

A SYNOPSIS OF MATRIX CAPABILITIES

Throughout the book, I have referred to the capabilities that a company needs to successfully execute a matrix organization. Because the discussions of these capabilities are spread throughout the chapters, I thought that it would be useful to bring them together in one place. You can then use them as a checklist or put each capability on a scale from high to low to survey the management. The survey can test how effective the leaders believe the company is at executing the capability. The following are the competencies and capabilities necessary for executing a matrix.

☐ **The company possesses high social capital or no silos**

The matrix runs on informal communication through personal networks characterized by high levels of trust.

☐ **People work effectively in teams across organizational boundaries.**

Matrix is inherently a team-based organization. Team members and leaders must raise problems, debate the issues, and work jointly to resolve them. These teams work across functions, countries, and businesses.

☐ **The teams are interconnected.**

As shown in Figure 10.2, the teams connect the different sides of the matrix. They prepare plans that become the rows and columns of the planning spreadsheets. Issues are discovered in the team process and escalated to the top team.

☐ **People are trained in the skills of team problem solving and conflict management.**

Much of the work in teams relates to addressing differ-ences and conflicts. The teams work best when people have a common set of skills and a common process for managing conflicts.

☐ **Managers in key roles are naturally collaborative, and they live the values.**

The company recruits, selects, develops, and promotes the types of people who will thrive in a matrix organization.

☐ **Managers in key roles can influence without authority.**

Power in the company is based on knowledge and competence. People in key positions have learned to exercise influence without authority.

☐ **Performance management is based on full and fair assessments of performance.**

The company takes the time to thoroughly assess all types of performance on a quantitative as well as a subjective basis.

☐ **There are multidimensional accounting systems to track multidimensional performance.**

The company can track and determine P&Ls for all relevant dimensions of the matrix. These data are available to the teams preparing and executing the plans. The system is a common source of data for all the teams.

☐ **The planning process is also the conflict resolution process.**

The planning process is the forum for gathering con-flicts and resolving them. The process vacuums up the disputes on a regular basis.

- [ ] **There is a spreadsheet planning process that aligns the goals of the different dimensions of the matrix.**

  Using a multidimensional accounting system, teams prepare plans, and the planning process arrives at shared targets and goals.

- [ ] **The leadership builds networks and values networkers.**

  The leaders use events, rotational assignments, and training as opportunities for network building. A manager's effective use of cross-unit relationships is valued in a full performance assessment.

- [ ] **The leadership ensures that roles, responsibilities, and interfaces are clearly defined.**

  Accountability can be maintained in a matrix organization by defining roles and responsibilities at the key interfaces. As described in Chapter Six, leaders can use RACI charts or definitions, as ABB did. What is important is that the definitions be discussed, debated, and understood.

- [ ] **Joint escalation processes are known and used intelligently.**

  Issues should be identified and escalated jointly. There can be too many or too few issues that are brought to the leadership team. (See Chapter Thirteen for more detail.) Often a planning process owner can gather and prioritize them.

- [ ] **Problems are jointly addressed.**

  Effective companies develop norms and values that support joint problem solving. When a problem arises, people say, "How can we work this out?" or "How can I help?" These responses are in contrast with "It's not my problem; *they* screwed up." In an effective matrix, finger pointing is unacceptable.

☐ **The health of the organization is monitored.**

Like any organization, a matrix can develop some weak spots and issues. The process owner for planning or HR may take the responsibility. The place to watch is roles that have two bosses. They are the canaries in the coal mine. When I assess a matrix organization, I always interview these people or hold a focus group with them.

☐ **A strong leadership team sets the example.**

Leadership is a team sport in a matrix—especially at the top. When the escalation process is working, this is where the tough issues come for resolution. The top team needs to make the tough calls and set an example for the rest of the organization.

Although there are probably some additional features, these are the ones that I look for in an effective matrix organization.

Epilogue

PERSONAL STORIES

The Uses and Abuses of the Matrix

Summer 2007 marked the fortieth anniversary of my introduction to matrix. This book is a result of my reflecting on these forty years. Initially I approached matrix as a scholar and wrote articles and books about it. In the late 1970s, I began giving public seminars on the subject. These seminars led to many consulting opportunities in many industries and in many countries. This book also resulted from all these experiences, which were based on my academic framework. In this Epilogue, I want to tell some stories, mostly about my consulting experiences. They will give a good picture of the evolution of a management concept—the matrix organization. The evolution of matrix very much parallels my own experience with it. The stories are arranged in the stages through which the concept of the matrix organization has passed.

Early Phase: "What Is a Matrix, Anyway?"

This early phase for me began in 1967 and ran until 1977. It was a period when everyone was trying to learn what this form of organization was and how it worked. The prevailing opinion was that matrix might work in aerospace but would not work in the commercial world. The thinking was that the government would pay for all the overhead and businesspeople would not. My position was agnostic, and I approached the subject as a researcher trying to learn about it. By far my most important experience was with the research project at Boeing's commercial airplane division.

Boeing, Summer 1967

In June 1967 I arrived in Seattle with two graduate students to spend the next three months assessing the commercial airplane division (CAD) of Boeing. At Boeing there were MIT graduates everywhere, and they had contracted with the dean of the Sloan School at MIT to do a research and consulting project for about three years. At the time, I was a young assistant professor at MIT. The project was to begin with an assessment of CAD; then the MIT professors and Boeing would choose and prioritize projects. It turned out that all the senior professors were busy that summer, so I was "asked" to go to Seattle. That assignment turned out to be one of the best things that ever happened to me.

The CAD made two full-time managers and a secretary available to work with me and the graduate students. These were senior managers and alumni of the Minute Man program, which, I came to learn, was very important, as it enabled us to conduct our project. As it turned out, all the important leaders of Boeing had been through the Minute Man program and had developed connections throughout the organization. These managers got us access to everyone and to all the data we wanted. Having this access and conducting interviews with all the key players made this project a great learning experience for me.

As the summer wore on, it wasn't clear who was having more difficulty, the CAD or me. I was clearly in over my head. I had never done an organization assessment before, and I was improvising as I went. The only reason I could do this was that I was from MIT. People automatically thought I knew what I was doing and were very cooperative. The CAD was struggling to make a program-function matrix work. It had historically used a functional structure to manage one or maybe two programs at a time. But as the jet aircraft market took off in the mid-1960s, Boeing had introduced the 737, the 747, and a prototype for the Supersonic Transport (SST). These development programs were added to the two ongoing production programs for the 707 and the 727. The CAD had four program managers, one each for the 707–727, the 737, the 747, and the SST, all reporting to the general manager of the division. They were joined by the three main functional VPs for engineering, manufacturing, and sales and marketing. So the struggle was for cooperation among the four program managers and the three functional managers; through our Boeing contacts, I had interviews with all of them. Their difficulties were a powerful lesson to me. Here was a situation where matrix was clearly the structure to use, but the resistance was equally strong.

The resistance came from the functions. They used to run the programs one at a time. Now there were five programs and a need to have a program manager for each one who would lie awake at night and worry about only that program. The functional managers were proud veterans of the airplane division, which had built the B-29; the B-52; the KC-135, which was then converted into Boeing's first commercial jet aircraft, the 707; and then struggled for four years to introduce the 727. They believed that a functional organization was the way that you managed airplane programs. The programs and program management structure came from the CEO, "T" Wilson. T, as he was known, was the program manager on Minute Man. The Minute Man program was the first program ever to come in ahead of schedule and under budget. The head of the CAD, the program managers, and other people in key positions in the CAD were all from the Minute Man program and from the aerospace side of Boeing.

The culture clash was enormous. It was not just function versus program. It was older functional airplane builder versus younger program-matrix aerospace competitor. The aerospace leaders came from the world of fixed-price incentive contracts. The old airplane builders came from the world of cost-plus contracts. They felt that it was normal to overrun the budget by 10 percent. The aerospace leaders, called space cadets by the airplane builders, got very nervous because a 10 percent overrun on the 747 program alone was equal to the net worth of the company. So they brought in all their program management tools and accounting systems to get control of the programs. These were seen as unnecessary overheads by the airplane builders.

The Minute Man clique carried the day. T Wilson insisted on holding reviews using program management reporting systems, disputes were resolved in favor of the program managers, and the VPs of engineering and manufacturing took early retirement. The CAD settled into a program-dominant matrix. The organizing principle of a strong program manager and accountability was stated in T Wilson's language as needing "one ass to kick." (This language has survived to today, though the part of the anatomy has changed, so today male managers want "one throat to choke." I have yet to hear a female manager use the expression.) The structure seemed entirely appropriate to me at the time, and does now, even in retrospect. The programs are large and long. You could join Boeing and spend your entire career on the 747 program. There were tight financial and schedule constraints. The champion of these goals was the program manager.

The two-year project taught me a lot, and not just about matrix. Certainly seeing and working with the CAD's matrix has proved invaluable to me. But I also began to develop my thinking about the Star Model. The program management tools and systems as well as the people were key to success. Boeing was also using a local consulting firm, whose name escapes me. That firm introduced me to the RACI charts. They were effective at defining the roles and responsibilities. I have used these RACI charts ever since. The project led to my first book (Galbraith, 1973), in which I discuss matrix, Boeing, and RACI charts.

R&D Managers Are Interested

The book became the basis for my teaching and executive course experience. At MIT, the R&D management course participants were always interested in matrix. We learned a lot from each other. In 1974, I followed my department chairman from MIT, Don Carroll, to the Wharton School. Don had been the project leader on the Boeing project and wanted me to join the management group at Wharton. This move set the stage for the next phase.

Matrix Takes Off and Becomes Trendy

In 1976, I was invited to participate in the program management course at the University of Michigan. I presented the "organization" part of the course and told the Boeing story. Following me came some people from Dow-Corning who gave a positive and enlightening story of their implementation of the matrix. Thus I began to sense a growing interest in the topic.

The Fad Begins

In 1978, the Wharton School began a partnership with the New York Management Center (NYMC). The partnership was to develop executive education courses using the Wharton faculty. I offered to do one on matrix organization. The NYMC did not like having the word "matrix" in the title. They liked "Project Management and Organization." So we scheduled two seminars for Chicago and New York. The Chicago seminar attracted twelve people. However, the ratings were very good. After a discussion, the NYMC and I decided to call the New York seminar "Matrix Management." One week later, the NYMC called and said, "We've struck a mother lode." It had one hundred reservations and was turning people away. So we quickly scheduled another. Eventually I was doing one seminar per month in all the major cities across the United States. We were attracting between fifty and eighty people per seminar.

It was at this time that I converted from an agnostic to a skeptic. I thought, "Surely, not all of these companies are candidates for matrix organizations." On the basis of my Boeing experience, I presented matrix as a difficult and challenging structure to implement. My message was "only use matrix if you have to." I still have people approach me today and thank me for talking them out of using a matrix. Most people did not heed my message, however.

Matrix Consulting

Some people who attended my seminars liked my message. They invited me to address their own management meetings. When this kind of presentation went well, the leadership would ask me to work with them to implement the matrix. One of the companies that I worked with was Intel. For three years, I worked with its leaders and learned a lot from the experience. Andy Grove was an insightful organization designer. He was also a great believer in matrix and in performance appraisals. He taught the course at Intel on giving performance appraisals. I adopted his thinking and added reward systems to my Star Model.

By 1979, I was getting more requests for my time than the academic rules would allow. So I took a two-year leave of absence from Wharton and consulted full-time. I loved it. Instead of giving lectures, now I was sitting around the table with managers problem-solving about their matrix. I resigned my position as full professor at Wharton to consult full-time. My academic colleagues thought I was crazy. In part they were correct. I have never regained my academic credibility. My consulting experience from 1979 to 1986 was seen by them as a waste of time that could have been spent writing articles for *Administrative Science Quarterly*.

Many of the experiences were great learning opportunities for me. Like Intel, projects at AT&T, Northwestern Bell, Northwestern Bank Corporation (now part of Wells Fargo), Exxon Research and Engineering, and others were good projects for me and for them. However, I was beginning to see the dark side of a trendy management concept.

The Abuse of Matrix

Along with these good projects came some not so good ones. A couple of HR people from NL Industries attended one of my seminars. They then approached me to work with them on implementing matrix at NL. NL was the former National Lead Company. With the decline of lead materials, the company diversified and became a conglomerate in all kinds of businesses. We set up a day with the three of us and the head of corporate HR at NL. I took the morning to explain what I thought matrix was about. After lunch, the head of HR said that he wanted to enlist my services to help him change his dotted-line relationship to the heads of HR in the businesses to a solid line. I asked, "How do we do this when standard practice in holding companies is for corporate staffs to have a dotted line?" He said, "Because matrix is the organization of the future, and NL needs to be in the forefront of the movement." He basically wanted to use the current positive view of matrix to bulldoze the opposition to allow him to do a power grab. After some discussion, we decided that I was not the person for the job. Situations like this one are common. Someone uses the popularity of a management concept like matrix or reengineering to exploit a situation for political advantage. These abuses invariably lead to skepticism and the eventual decline of a useful concept.

Another situation resulted when I was invited to present matrix to Aramco (the Arabian American Oil Company). At the time, Aramco was owned by the Saudi government but was staffed and run by people from the Western oil companies. For years, the Saudis asked that Saudi nationals be moved into positions of power in the company. Each time, the Western oil companies said that the Saudi people were not ready for such responsibility. Then, after the 1973 oil embargo, the Saudis became more forceful and said "Promote them now!" So the oil companies did promote them, but they also left the Westerners in their current positions. The result was two people in every position, one Saudi and one Westerner. The clear intention was to keep the Westerners in control. When the Saudis questioned the staffing, the Westerners said that it was a matrix organization—the latest trend in organizing business. So they told the Saudis that they could get this expert from MIT to come over and explain it to them.

When I arrived and found out what the situation was, I said, "That's not a matrix." My hosts said, "Look, you know that, we know that, but they [the Saudis] don't. Give us a hand." So I felt that I had to do something. Finally we agreed on a training program that focused on managing when working with two bosses. I asked one of the Americans what it was like to work with two-in-a-box. He said that in his case it wasn't too bad. His partner did not work very hard and liked to travel. He claimed that most of the Saudis liked to travel outside of Saudi Arabia and loved the chance to drink some Scotch. So his partner was gone two weeks a month. I think that the most powerful person in the company was the head of export sales, who arranged all the travel. I lost track of the situation after I left. I assume that the Saudis saw the ruse and eliminated the two-boss system. Eventually the Saudis took over and now own and run the company. So there appears to be no limit to the ways that a popular concept can be used or abused for political purposes.

Sometimes matrix was the appropriate structure, but it was implemented poorly. I discovered an example when I was invited to hold a workshop at Wright-Patterson (W-P) airbase in Dayton, Ohio. In the late 1970s, the size of the military was being reduced. When all the people reported to program managers, a lot of duplication took place. So a number of military installations centralized such activities as the engineering function and shared people across programs. This change was an appropriate use of the matrix organization.

The commanding officer at W-P had read in an airline magazine about matrix organizations and their effectiveness. On the next Monday morning, he convened his staff and announced

the move to a matrix. All the program managers were to transfer their engineers to the central engineering function. The
program managers at W-P were two- and three-star gener-
als. One of them was a three-star who was the program manager for the B-2 bomber. Being in the military, however, they
saluted and complied—well, almost. They transferred some of
their engineers to the central function. But most of the really
good engineers they kept, giving them new titles like cost controller and project scheduler. The central engineering leaders
discovered the deception and began arguing with the program
managers. The dispute got to be pretty heated, and to settle the
argument they decided to bring me in to give a lecture on how
matrix structures work.

So this was the context when I arrived. I was totally unaware
of the circumstances. Further, many in the audience thought
that it was my idea that led to the changes in the first place.
Well, I have never faced a more hostile audience. Within an
hour, we sorted out that I had had nothing to do with the reorganization decision. But it was still a difficult group. I think that
in the end the program managers kept control of the top engineers. This example is probably the most blatant but not the
only one in which a leader tried to install a matrix. There were
many who jumped on the bandwagon and wanted to get their
matrix up and running quickly. These organizations had few of
the capabilities that support a matrix. It is no wonder that many
of these efforts did not succeed. When increasing numbers of
bandwagon failures begin singing the refrain, "We tried matrix
organization, and it doesn't work," decline of the fad begins.

The Phase of Decline

I've come to believe that once a hot concept hits the airline
magazines, it is the beginning of the end. All the wrong people
will use it for all the wrong reasons. People then quickly read
the political winds and shift from the trendy bandwagon to the

"it doesn't work" bandwagon. The concept then becomes a scapegoat for people's poor performance. It also becomes a tool for people trying to earn credibility. These people then issue statements that pander to managers' common beliefs.

The best example of scapegoating was at Texas Instruments (TI) about 1980. TI had been built by Pat Haggerty through the 1970s. He had received a lot of notoriety for his Objectives, Strategies and Tactics (OST) system. OST was basically an industry matrix that was laid across the TI business units (then called product-customer centers) and guided decisions about capital and R&D investments. Pat was a tough manager with a heart, who knew how to run a matrix. When Pat retired, Mark Shepard and Fred Bucy took over. These guys were just plain tough. They were command-and-controllers who took no criticism and could not manage a healthy debate. As TI declined, one of their turnaround moves was to get rid of OST. By getting rid of OST, they said, they were scrapping the matrix and becoming lean and mean. When large numbers of people believe that matrix doesn't work, leaders can eliminate it and appear to be taking meaningful actions toward a turnaround. Shepard and Bucy's move was a cover story in *BusinessWeek* and was announced with fanfare to Wall Street analysts. Presumably it was the matrix that was holding TI back.

The change did the company little good. It certainly became more mean. The real reason behind TI's decline was that it was being beaten in semiconductors by Intel and in consumer electronics by Sony and the Japanese. It wasn't long before Shepard and Bucy were out. Getting rid of the matrix merely bought them some time before their eventual demise.

The real death blow to the matrix came with the publication of *In Search of Excellence*, by Peters and Waterman. In the book and in their many speeches, they listed the virtues of the excellent companies, such as "close to the customer," and then capped their presentation with "and none of them had a matrix organization." Of course, I knew that the statement was false.

I had worked with three of the excellent companies, Boeing, DEC, and Intel, to implement their matrix organizations. I also knew that Fluor and Bechtel used matrix organization to run their global engineering and construction business. But Peters and Waterman had the spotlight now, and I did not.

I have often wondered why they added that statement about matrix. They didn't have to. The content of their book about being excellent could stand by itself. Peters and Waterman made some good points. I can only believe that they added it to earn credibility with their audiences. They were not well known when the book first appeared. And by the time it hit the scene, there were many people in their audiences who had had bad experiences with matrix. So when Tom Peters announced that the excellent companies didn't use matrix, his statement resonated with them. Thus the study of excellent companies sealed the case: matrix didn't work.

The Stealth Matrix Phase

Companies like Intel continued to use matrix. Most R&D labs continued to use matrix as the accepted way to run a lab. But most conversations about matrix stopped. And when new implementations occurred, the designers called them something other than matrix. No leader wanted to expose themselves to the ridicule that would result. It was the period of the stealth matrix.

In 1986, I returned to the academic world in part. I joined Ed Lawler's Center for Effective Organizations at the University of Southern California. The Center had a mission to do "useful research." It was an oasis in the academic world where it is more important to have a new idea than a useful one. I taught executive courses part-time and worked on projects part-time. One project was with Kodak, a long-time sponsor of the Center. It was a typical project for me. McKinsey was there first to develop the corporate strategy and had left an organization chart to implement that strategy. I have always worked the McKinsey aftermarket. The photographic film division was not sure how to implement the structure and asked me to help.

When I arrived at Kodak Park, the managers described to me their "shared resource organization." They had several photographic film product lines, all of which shared the big silver halide manufacturing center. When I saw and heard their presentation, I said, "Oh, it's a matrix." Very quickly they corrected me: "No, no. This is not a matrix. McKinsey was very clear. This is a shared resource organization." I very quickly determined that this was not an argument worth having. I pulled out my Star Model and went to work with my matrix experiences and tools.

Kodak was one of many companies using a stealth matrix. A lot of these stealth matrix designs were implemented with an emphasis on teams. We had labels like empowered teams, Team Taurus at Ford, and heavyweight product teams. When the heavyweight product manager was added to lead cross-functional teams, it is pretty clear that we were talking about a product-function matrix organization. It was this emphasis on cross-functional product teams driven by shorter and shorter product development cycles that brought the introduction of matrix to business units. Richard Anderson wrote an article in *Business Horizons* in 1994 called "Matrix Redux." Its subtitle was "Don't Look Now, but the Organizational Fad of the 1970s Is on the Way Back."

I think that the ABB experience from 1986 to 1998 was two steps forward and one step backward for the matrix. The positive public position that Percy Barnevik took on matrix and ABB's success helped a lot. People asked why ABB was successful and found that the clear role definitions and supporting accounting and planning systems were key enablers of success. People began to appreciate a Star Model view. However, when ABB abandoned the matrix in 1998 and subsequently experienced economic difficulty, it could no longer serve as a positive example. There were few public advocates like Barnevik, but there were still those willing to publicly trash the matrix and use it as a scapegoat.

Today: Matrix Out of the Closet

I believe today that managers adopt the matrix when circumstances call for one. Whether they call it a matrix or a heavyweight product team is irrelevant. So, as I mentioned in the text, the two-dimensional matrix is a solved problem. Although there has been no public pronouncement, the corporate function–business unit matrix is standard practice. Business units that compete through new product development use a product-function or service-function matrix. R&D labs have always been run using matrix structures. There is little reason to make a big deal about them, however.

Today the challenge is to implement the three- and four-dimensional matrix across international borders. There are many managers around the world who have experienced and are experiencing the negatives of working in these structures. For many of these managers, experience has taught them that matrix doesn't work. They can have these beliefs reinforced by articles in the *Wall Street Journal* titled "Office Democracies: How Many Bosses Can One Person Have?" (Sandberg, 2005). Journalists can find willing readers to laugh at or resonate with horror stories of people with five bosses. It is still easy to find examples of dysfunctional matrix organizations.

I can also find people who see the matrix structures as a natural consequence of working in a complex business. I recall the business leader at American Express who had eighteen lines reporting to him, most of them dotted. When asked if this was difficult, he said, "No. It's all about relationships. I take the time to build relationships with all of them. I treat them all like members of my team. I keep them all informed. It's all based on relationships." Then there is A. G. Lafley, the CEO of P&G. When asked why P&G was doing so well, he described several factors, one of which was P&G's unique organization. It was a four-dimensional front-back model. So as more companies start to perfect these multidimensional structures, more people will have positive experiences with them. At some point, the tide will turn in favor of matrix. Then it will be neither a fad nor a pariah but a normal way of doing business.

To summarize my view, if you are a multibusiness company, you will experience the corporate function–business unit matrix. If you do business in multiple countries, you will experience the three-dimensional international matrix. If you are in the B-2-B world, you will probably have global customers wanting global service; the four-dimensional front-back structure is probably in your future. Complex businesses will need to be managed through complex organizations like the matrix.

References

Bartlett, C., and Ghoshal, S. "Matrix Management: Not a Structure, a Frame of Mind." *Harvard Business Review*, July 1, 1990. Reprint 90401.

Bartlett, C., and McLean, A. "GE's Talent Machine: The Making of a CEO." Case no. 9-304-049. Boston: Harvard Business School Publishing, 2004.

Beer, M., and Nohria, N. *Breaking the Code of Change.* Boston: Harvard Business School Press, 2000.

Berry, L. "The Collaborative Organization: Leadership Lessons from Mayo Clinic." *Organizational Dynamics*, 2004, 33(3), 228–242.

Bryan, L., and Joyce, C. "The 21st-Century Organization." *McKinsey Quarterly*, No. 3, 2005, pp. 25–33.

Bunker, B., and Albans, B. *Large Group Interventions.* San Francisco: Jossey-Bass, 1997.

Clark, K., and Wheelwright, S. *The Product Development Challenge.* Boston: Harvard Business School Press, 1995.

Davis, S., and Lawrence, P. *Matrix.* Reading, Mass.: Addison-Wesley, 1977.

Doz, Y. *Government Control and Multinational Strategic Management.* New York: Praeger, 1988.

Eccles, R., and Crane, D. *Doing Deals: Investment Banks at Work.* Boston: Harvard Business School Press, 1988.

Fayol, H. *General and Industrial Management: Henri Fayol's Classic Revised by Irwin Gray.* Belmont, Calif.: Lake, 1987. (Originally published 1949.)

Galbraith, J. *Designing Complex Organizations.* Reading, Mass.: Addison-Wesley, 1973.

Galbraith, J. *Organization Design.* Reading, Mass.: Addison-Wesley, 1977.

Galbraith, J. *Competing with Flexible Lateral Organizations.* (2nd ed.) Reading, Mass.: Addison-Wesley, 1994.

Galbraith, J. *Designing the Global Corporation.* San Francisco: Jossey-Bass, 2000.

Galbraith, J. *Designing Organizations: An Executive Guide to Strategy, Structure, and Process.* (Rev. ed.) San Francisco: Jossey-Bass, 2002.

Galbraith, J. *Designing the Customer-Centric Organization: A Guide to Strategy, Structure, and Process.* San Francisco: Jossey-Bass, 2005.

Galbraith, J., Downey, D., and Kates, A. *Designing Dynamic Organizations: A Hands-on Guide for Leaders at All Levels*. New York: American Management Association, 2002.

Galbraith, J., Lawler, E. E. III, and Associates. *Organizing for the Future*. San Francisco: Jossey-Bass, 1993.

Hemp, P., and Stewart, T. "Leading Change When Business Is Good." *Harvard Business Review*, Dec. 1, 2004, pp. 61–70.

Henderson, R. "The Evolution of Integrative Capability: Innovation in Cardiovascular Drug Discovery." *Industrial and Corporate Change*, 1994a, *3*(3), 607–630.

Henderson, R. "Managing Innovation in the Information Age." *Harvard Business Review*, Jan. 1, 1994b. Reprint 94105.

Hofstede, G. H. *Culture's Consequences*. Thousand Oaks, Calif.: Sage, 1984.

Lorsch, J. "McKinsey & Co." Case no. 9-402-014. Boston: Harvard Business School Publishing, 2001.

Lorsch, J., and Tierney, T. *Aligning the Stars: How to Succeed When Professionals Drive Results*. Boston: Harvard Business School Press, 2002.

Maister, D. "The One-Firm Firm: What Makes It Successful." *Sloan Management Review*, Fall 1985, pp. 3–13.

Maister, D., and Walker, J. "The One-Firm Firm Revisited." http://davidmaister. com/articles/1/101, 2006.

Malknight, T. "Eli Lilly, 1998 (A): Strategic Challenges." Case no. 9-399-173. Boston: Harvard Business School Publishing, 1999a.

Malknight, T. "Eli Lilly, 1998 (B): Emerging Global Organization." Case no. 9-399-174. Boston: Harvard Business School Publishing, 1999b.

Michaels, E., Handfield-Jones, H., and Axelrod, B. *The War for Talent*. Boston: Harvard Business School Press, 2001.

Peck, M., and Scherer, F. *The Weapons Acquisition Process*. Boston: Harvard Business School Press, 1962.

Peters, T., and Waterman, R. *In Search of Excellence*. New York: Harpers, 1982.

Pucik, V., and Zalan, T. "Rebuilding ABB (A)." Case no. IMD-3-1797. 2007. Available from IMD (www.imd.ch).

Sandberg, J. "Office Democracies: How Many Bosses Can One Person Have?" *Wall Street Journal*, Nov. 22, 2005, p. B1.

Spangler, W. S., Kreulen, J., and Newswanger, J. "Machines in the Conversation: Detecting Themes and Trends in Informal Communication Streams." www.research.ibm.com/journal/sj/454/spangler.html, 2006.

Thomke, S. "Eli Lilly and Company: Drug Development Strategy (A)." Case no. 9-698-010. Boston: Harvard Business School Publishing, 1997.

Wheelwright, S. "Eli Lilly: The Evista Project." Case no. 9-699-016. Boston: Harvard Business School Publishing, 1999.

About the Author

Dr. Jay Galbraith, an affiliated research scientist at the Center for Effective Organizations at the University of Southern California, and Professor Emeritus at the International Institute for Management Development in Lausanne, Switzerland, is an internationally recognized expert on organization design.

He is the president and founder of Galbraith Management Consultants, an international consulting firm that specializes in solving strategy and organizational design challenges across corporate, business unit, and international levels. Over forty years of research and practical applications give Galbraith a breadth of experience that few management consultants can claim. His clientele range from small manufacturing companies to large global firms operating in virtually every industry. Galbraith's theories on gaining a significant competitive advantage through organization design and customer-centricity have been implemented by top-level executives throughout the world.

Galbraith, creator of the widely used Star Model™, has written numerous publications, including *Designing the Customer-Centric Organization*, *Designing the Global Corporation*, *Designing Dynamic Organizations*, and *Designing Organizations: An Executive Guide to Strategy, Structure and Process*. *Designing Your Organization* (with Amy Kates) is a hands-on workbook and toolbox for practitioners.

In addition, Galbraith is regularly sought after for his expert opinion by the media, including *BusinessWeek*, the *Wall Street Journal*, *Fortune*, *The Economist*, and the *Financial Times*.

For more information, please visit www.jaygalbraith.com.

Index